The School Lunchbox Cookbook

Text design: Nancy Freeborn
Illustrations: Eileen Hine

Library of Congress Cataloging-in-Publication Data

Jacobs, Miriam
The school lunchbox cookbook / Miriam Jacobs.—1st ed.
p. cm.
Includes bibliographical references and index.
ISBN 0-7627-2757-8
1. Lunchbox cookery. I. Title.

TX735.J28 2003
641.5'3—dc21

2003056370

Manufactured in the United States of America
First Edition/First Printing

The School Lunchbox COOKBOOK

Miriam Jacobs

GUILFORD, CONNECTICUT

For

Sarah, Abigail, and Adam,

who ate all their peanut-butter-on-whole-wheat sandwiches without complaints and grew up to be people I am proud of every day

Contents

Acknowledgments

I want to thank David Emblidge, acquisitions editor at The Globe Pequot Press, with whom I discussed the need for this book for many years and who then took the lead to make it happen, and Cary Hull, project editor, whose patience and dedication to detail saw this book through to the end. I also thank my friends, in particular Carole Owens, Sally Greco, Donna Bartell, and Stephanie Hebb, who generously gave me recipe ideas for this collection. I thank my kids who for years were my private experimental lab animals, on whom I tried out my imaginative cooking and my boring sense of good nutrition. I know I lied to you about dishes that contained the dreaded zucchini and tofu, but you liked them and it was for your own good. And, of course, my mom, Selma Jacobs, who fed her family with imagination and attention to nutrition. Thank you, as always.

About This Book

Lunchtime at school ought to be an enjoyable break from the rigors of classroom work. Kids love to socialize, and the lunch table is a favorite spot for that. At the same time, the school cafeteria is like a gas station where necessary refueling takes place. Growing children, from kindergartners to high schoolers, burn calories at an amazing rate. To feel good, stay lively, and perform well for the balance of the day, kids need a healthy lunch. The catch is that to get them to eat a nutritious lunch, it has to be not only interesting but efficient, too. School lunchtime is not a leisurely affair; on the contrary, speed is of the essence.

The good news is, as you will see in this book, there are loads of convenient and economical ways to succeed at giving your kids school lunches that not only will they love to eat (though maybe not with the attentiveness of a food connoisseur!) but that will nourish them as well.

Still, the inspiration for writing a book of recipes for school lunches was, alas, not an entirely happy one. Although it's true that thinking about all the healthy and delicious options there are for school lunches for kids is a wonderfully pleasant and amusing exercise, at the same time I was responding to some distressing news. In the last two decades, as the American fast-food industry has burgeoned and as the number of households with two working parents or with only one parent has also multiplied, the attention paid to the quality and variety of our kids' school lunches has declined precipitously. We just aren't feeding this generation's kids as well as our moms fed us.

There are other factors at work here, of course, not the least of which are television and home computers and their capacity to render kids or adults so passive that they rarely get any healthy exercise. But what our kids eat for lunch at school is one important element in their health, and its poor quality has become a national scandal. The obesity problem and related health concerns (early diabetes, for one) among a rapidly growing percentage of our children are scary and depressing. So I'll explore in more detail the roots and causes of this decline in the quality of American school lunches. I'll also look at cultural and economic factors and try to lay out some ways that families can combat the tide of bad temptations toward fatty and otherwise unhealthy foods or passive lifestyles.

Basic Assumptions

I realize that all kids are not created equal (in terms of taste buds), so I have written these recipes to have mild uncomplicated flavors and to use standard and widely available ingredients. Your children will have their own quirks, and your household might be used to different foods than mine was. If you eat traditional Indian or Mexican food at home, I am sure your kids were accustomed to the heat of cayenne in their food by the time they went to school. My children, to my great frustration, never liked their food spicy until they grew up. If your kids want parsley sprinkled on their food, like hot sauce, devour artichoke hearts, and look kindly on eggplant, more power to you both!

This collection of recipes is meant as a set of suggestions; they are ideas to help you get inspired about making healthy, nourishing lunches. They are not in the least bit meant to be the final word on anything, and I'm sure you'll create lots of exciting variations of your own.

I have designed these to be sturdy recipes. A little more of this and a little less of that will not make or break the end result: We are not trying to win a gourmet cooking contest here, folks; it's just food, remember?

Boring but Healthy? NOT!

This book is designed to help you create a healthy, fast, delicious, homemade lunch for your child to eat at school. I happen to think that is important.

When my kids were in school, I was frustrated by the task of making their lunches. I made, and my kids made for themselves, huge numbers of peanut-butter-on-whole-wheat-bread sandwiches. They ate lots of carrot sticks, and for snacks they often had a piece of fruit. I took great pride in making good dinners for us all, but somehow the extra effort of thinking of something original for them to take to school for lunch was often too much. (I really wish I had had this book when my kids were young!) However, though their school lunches might have been less than inspiring, our visits to the doctor were very infrequent.

These are not diet recipes, and they do not address specific allergy issues. What I have attempted is to put together a collection of fun, easy suggestions for giving your child real food in his or her lunchbox. My core philosophy is that if you feed your children normal, wholesome, healthy food on a regular basis, if you have them move and play a lot outside, and if you limit their access to junk food and soda, they'll be just fine.

Some of the recipes in this book also appear in my *Brown Bag Lunch Cookbook* for adults. The versions here, though, take into consideration children's tastes and food preferences.

I had my three children—two girls and a boy—to learn on, so these recipes come from the heart and are loaded with the benefits of practical experience. But before we get to the recipes, I'd like to walk you through all the practical knowledge I have gathered—kitchen and supermarket wisdom, as it were—pertaining to planning and preparing convenient, healthy, and tasty school lunches your kids will go for.

Straight Talk
about Kids and
Their Lunches

Principles and Strategies for Healthy School Lunches

Keeping Lunch Safe

Obviously it is critical that the lunch you pack is safe to eat! Keep these common sense precautions in mind.

Food spoils because food-borne pathogens, aka germs, grow on food surfaces in great numbers. The two keys to preventing this condition are: keep the food as clean as possible to begin with, and then give the germs the least friendly environment in which to multiply.

Pathogens grow most slowly in very cold or very hot environments, so the goal is to keep cold foods cold and hot foods hot until they are eaten. This precaution starts in the kitchen: Place food back in the refrigerator as soon as it is practical after lunch preparations. If you are making a chicken salad from the chicken left over from dinner, do that before you do the dinner dishes, so that the chicken salad can get cold right away.

Scrub well and clean all fruits and vegetables. They may look clean coming into the house from the supermarket, but that does not mean they are fit to eat.

Keeping clean the school lunchbox itself as well as any containers you use to pack a lunch in is vital. Wipe clean the interior of the lunchbox once a week with a paper towel dipped in a very dilute bleach solution (1 teaspoon in a gallon of water).

Teach your child the importance of washing hands before eating. After a thousand repetitions of this concept, your child will remember most of the time. My nineteen-year-old son recently took a course in food handling given by the department of health. When I asked him what he had learned, he told me that the thing that had made the biggest impression on him was the necessity to wash his hands. I nearly fainted! After all those years of repetition, I was still not the one to succeed in impressing this point on him.

Frozen juice boxes are a great way to keep a lunch cold in a lunchbox (by lunchtime, the drink will defrost). So are ice packs, of course, but you might have to be prepared to lose a few here and there. You might also want to recycle well-cleaned, small water bottles. Fill them half full with water or a beverage, place the cap on loosely so some air can escape, and freeze them. In the morning fill them up the rest of the way. (A fully frozen bottle might not be sufficiently defrosted in the few hours between packing the food and lunchtime.) Be sure to place the cap on securely before you pack the bottle in the lunchbox.

Consider buying an insulated lunchbox to keep lunch cold—or hot—longer. However, your child may be unwilling to take one of those bigger boxes to school: lunchboxes are a playground and cafeteria status symbol, and it is hard to argue "germ multiplication" versus "but they'll make fun of me." You'll have to compromise and do everything you can to keep the lunch cold or hot by using the suggestions above.

Rinse a thermos with boiling water before you fill it with hot stew or soup. That way it will really stay warm. Warn your small child that the soup will be hot and to eat it carefully.

What Your Child NEEDS

This short overview of necessary nutrients is in no way complete, and I recommend that you get more information if you are interested. See the Resources at the end of this book. Bear in mind also that no food is exclusively a protein or a carbohydrate or a fat.

Your Child NEEDS Fats

Do not, unless you are under strict doctor's orders and constant supervision, put your child on a low-fat diet. Don't assume that you can help your children by simply eliminating fat from their diets. You might actually be hurting them. Current guidelines from the National Cholesterol Education Program recommend that your children ought to get 30 percent of their calories from fat. And it should not all be unsaturated fat either. Cholesterol in food is necessary for infants and children to grow well. Good fats are absolutely essential to children's growth and health.

Low-fat diets actually can have the opposite effect you are looking for. They might well make your child overeat because he or she is not feeling satisfied! Most likely what is making your child fat is consuming too much white sugar, white flour, soda, and other empty calories; and not exercising enough.

What you ought to control are the kinds of fats your child eats, and you'll want to eliminate as far as possible all unhealthy fats such as trans fats, which are mainly a product of the partial hydrogenation of vegetable oils. Olive oil is the best choice for salad dressings, and moderate amounts of butter are your best choice for spreading on bread and for use in baking. Eggs and the fat in meat and fish will also provide your child with fat, and in reasonable amounts and in an overall healthy and balanced diet, will not harm him or her.

Your Child NEEDS Proteins

Proteins are the building blocks of the body, which needs them for growth and repair in countless different ways. An adequate supply is necessary for normal growth, for the formation of hormones, for the process of blood clotting, and for thousands of other processes. Protein does not raise the blood sugar levels the way refined carbohydrates do and therefore does not spike your child's energy with the inevitable drop later.

Many teenagers, mostly girls, are becoming vegetarians. If this is a short-term experiment, you don't need to do much and might as well support it. After all, it can be an indication of a child's first attempt to take charge of his or her own diet. But if your child is serious about vegetarianism, make sure he or she knows how to balance out the intake of food to get adequate protein. Get a respected book on vegetarianism to get the right information. (See Resources.)

If you, the parent, are a vegetarian, I am sure you have done your research concerning your need for protein. Raising a healthy vegetarian child is no mean feat, and I will assume that with your health care provider you are making sure that you are on top of this issue, especially regarding the need for absorbable vitamin B_{12}.

Protein options for lunch include shaved meats such as roast beef, turkey, ham, and chicken; hard-boiled eggs; cheese, sliced or in cubes or string cheese; yogurt (with live cultures); cottage cheese; nut butters such as peanut or cashew; hummus or bean dips; or stews or soups with meats and beans. Milk is also a source of protein, if your child is able to digest it.

Your Child NEEDS Carbohydrates

Carbohydrates are necessary for energy and fiber and the many vitamins and minerals they contain.

However, not all carbohydrates are equal. By the time the food industry does its magic with our grains, fruits, and vegetables, these foods are totally transformed. It is true, for instance, that sugar is a carbohydrate, but it will not give you the nutrients of sugar the way an apple will. Good, dense carbohydrates are whole wheat bread, whole wheat pita bread, whole wheat bagels, tortillas, potatoes, brown rice, beans, and whole wheat pasta. All fruits and vegetables contain primarily (though not only) carbohydrates and are absolutely essential to supply necessary vitamins, minerals, and other food factors as well. No pill, however splendid the multivitamin might be, can ever replace the perfect balance of nutrients Mother Nature placed in fruits and vegetables. For a good list of vegetables and fruits, please look at the introductions the Fruits and Salads chapters.

What your child does not need is white sugar and white flour. Though these substances start out as foods, they are regularly stripped of every conceivable useful nutrient by the commercial food industry. In "enriched" white flour, some few (cheaply and synthetically made) vitamins have been added back in to compensate for the dozens of vitamins, minerals, and other food factors that have been leached and bleached out. There is probably no more significant change that you can make to improve your child's health than to cut out refined sugars in all forms. The main way that refined sugars are making their way into our diet right now is through the addition of corn syrup to a stunning array of foods, from soda to tomato ketchup. Read food labels carefully, look up the ingredients you don't understand, and don't be a passive, misled consumer! This book is not the place for me to tell you of all the ways that sugar harms your child, but the books listed in the Resources will give you a good start.

Your Child NEEDS Vitamins, Minerals, and Antioxidants

It seems that every month scientists "discover" a new something that we ought to eat to keep us healthy. You sometimes wonder how all the previous generations ever got by!

There is a much easier way to keep track of all the stuff your body needs: Eat colorful foods and limit foods that are white and beige. In

What Color Is Your Diet, Dr. David Heber explains that different groups of fruits and vegetables have different plant chemicals in them that will protect your body in different ways. I highly recommend his informative book, and in the introduction to the Salads chapter, I give a few of Dr. Heber's tips and examples.

Your Child NEEDS Water

Water—plain old water—is what your child needs. Soda is never necessary and should be a treat, not a normal part of a child's diet. If you give your child juice, look at the label to see that it is pure juice and not a sugary drink with a little bit of token juice added to it. If your child's excess weight is an issue, you might also want to read the calorie count on the juice boxes as juice is very high in calories. You might want to negotiate with your child to see if instead of a cup of apple juice he or she would go for water and an apple, which is much healthier and much more filling.

Learn from Take-Out Food: Don't Be Its Slave

Though take-out dinners are wonderfully convenient and a fast-food meal once in a while is perfectly fine, is eating junk food on a regular basis really meeting your family's needs, nutritionally and emotionally?

Going out to eat does not really save time. With some advance thought and planning, it is much faster to prepare a simple meal at home. You would do well to learn from fast-food restaurants. Why do you think a McDonalds or Kentucky Fried Chicken restaurant can serve you a meal as quickly as it does? Do you think it first puts up the water to boil potatoes for your fries once you order them? Do you think it starts washing the lettuce when you order a salad? Of course not! In the food business, as in every business, preparation is the mark of a professional. Planning and cooking ahead will make a huge difference not only in the nutrition you and your family receive, but also in your peace of mind.

Planning a Lunch: So, What Will We Eat?

Lunches are served in schools all around the world, and not all children are presented with the same dilemmas North American kids are. According to Ellen Ruppel Shell, codirector of the Knight Center for Science and Medical Journals at Boston University (*New York Times,* February 2003, page 12), the lunches served in countries as diverse as

South Korea and Russia are much more nutritious and appetizing than the fare most American kids are offered at school. To make matters worse, your kids, most likely, have the option of refusing this substandard, bland cafeteria fare for the tastier but nutritionally poor junk food and soda that many schools now provide because they get subsidies from the fast-food purveyors!

Sit down with your child and make a plan together. You need to get yourself and your child educated about good school lunches. Boys and girls must start to understand that the way they feel and look is directly related to the food they eat. If you want to blame the school for bad nutrition in the cafeteria, take that complaint to the PTA or to the school board. It is much, much better, in talking with your child, simply to decide that you two, together, will come up with a better solution. Kids love to make lists. You can teach them all about good organization and spelling, too, while the lunch plans develop. Is it "chocolate" or "chawkolat"? The most important lesson, though, is that they get a sense of what it means to be responsible for themselves, with your help.

If your child would like to eat the school lunch once in a while, get the month's schedule (often available on the Internet) and discuss the options at the beginning of the month. Decide which days will be good to bring lunch from home. Highlight the days when lunch will be bought at school. If you want to be really prepared, wrap money for lunch in little plastic baggies to have ready on those days. Place them in a special bowl close to the door; that way you avoid the morning madness of trying to find the right change.

Now make a schedule together for the lunch meals you're going to prepare yourselves, and make a shopping list at the same time. See what treats are still in the freezer, and plan to make one more batch of muffins that week to keep your supply replenished. Make sure you have the ingredients for items to be prepared well in advance. If not, put them on the shopping list.

I suggest that you make a similar plan for breakfasts and dinners, which again will give you a great measure of control and peace of mind. For the days when nobody is home at the same time and everybody is eating on the run, instead of take-out burgers, plan to make a large bowl of soup or minestrone, which can be kept warm in a Crock-Pot, and a large chef salad. Sunday supper with the family can be a simple dish that can be in the oven a long time, such as a roast surrounded with root vegetables, rather than a last-minute decision for a delivered pizza.

Making a large batch of pasta one night gives you leftovers for pasta vegetable salad two days later. Placing the ingredients in your Crock-Pot the night before and starting it in the morning means that you come home to a warm meal ready to eat the moment you step in the door. And, ah, the aroma!

Making this sort of plan also means a huge savings: Take-out food is never as cheap as what you can make at home. At the back end, you'll be saving money, too, because your healthier family will spend less on cold remedies and doctors' bills.

Making a plan enables you to keep track of your family's nutrition, and it will pay dividends for the rest of your life and their lives in bodies that have been well nourished and built.

Remember Your Favorites

Keep a list of foods both you and your kids decide are yummy and healthy. I have so many times "forgotten" a really good recipe that we all liked. A blackboard, white board, or a special notebook are good ways of keeping track of evolving tastes and preferences. Make lists in the five basic categories: sandwiches, fruits and veggies, snacks, desserts, and drinks. You might be surprised what your children will and will not eat, but you are much better off knowing this before they throw out or trade their food at school. Use this list to make a weekly plan.

Slow Down

The idea that eating is an experience that we have to do as quickly as possible is bizarre to me. Speed is admirable when it is connected with concepts such as doing taxes, tooth extraction, or waiting in line at the supermarket checkout. But eating is neither painful nor boring; it is a joyful, sensual, healing, nourishing, social experience. So why is speed so essential? If you and your family are wolfing down meals, trying to fit them in your schedules and not sitting down together, maybe you need to look at your priorities.

Eat Breakfast

I know families who get up half an hour earlier than they did before, just so that they can all sit down in the morning and have a simple breakfast together. This does not necessarily mean a lot of extra work. Cooking oatmeal in a slow cooker overnight ensures an automatic warm bowl in the morning. The bread maker you were so enthusiastic about a few years ago could be dusted off and a fresh little loaf of bread could be waiting for you all when you wake up. A child can be in charge of setting the breakfast table in the evening, after supper, so that it is ready for you in the morning. Eggs can be cracked the night before and sitting in the blender bowl in the refrigerator waiting to be whipped and made into a quick omelet. Add a little chopped, leftover spinach salad from the night before and you have a gourmet meal as fast as it takes for you to wait at the fast-food drive up window.

Sending a child off to school with a proper breakfast in his or her belly is guaranteed to help control weight and to foster better concentration, too.

Eating Breakfast on the Run

For those mornings when breakfast just does not work out, be sure to hand your child something nutritious to eat on the run. Studies show, and every teacher will tell you, that your child learns better on a full tummy. You might want to make little snack bags ahead of time with cereal, dried fruit, and some nuts—easy things they can eat on the run. Homemade (healthy!) muffins with a piece of cheese are also great to grab and eat. Send along an extra small juice box, milk box, or water bottle to wet their whistles.

Try It Out at Home First

Do not send a mystery food to school with your child: The chances of it ending up in the garbage bin are close to 100 percent unless he or she can figure out a way to trade it. If you want to introduce a new food, do it at home, so you can monitor the kids' reactions. If they hate it at home, they won't eat it away from home either. If it is too salty or too hot, make the adjustment, try it at home again, and make sure your kids know this is the new and improved version in their lunchbox.

The Freezer Is Your Friend

Yes, you can freeze sandwiches ahead of time, but you cannot freeze all sandwich fillings successfully. I would not freeze sandwiches for more than one or two months. Experiment with some sandwiches yourself and take them to work, so that you can be sure the taste and texture will be to your own satisfaction. Snacks, such as muffins, can also be frozen. The following lists will help you decide what can or cannot be frozen.

What you *cannot* freeze:
Eggs (as in egg salad)
Fresh fruits, with a few exceptions (see the Fruits chapter)
Greens such as lettuce, celery, and so on
Mayonnaise
Potatoes
Tomatoes
Yogurt

What you *can* freeze:
Breads, bagels, and rolls (slice bagels and rolls first)
Cream cheese
Hard cheeses such as cheddar, Swiss, and so on
Hummus
Jelly and jam
Ketchup
Muffins
Mustard
Peanut and other nut butters
Pickle relish
Sliced meats such as chicken, turkey, and so on

General Hints and Ideas

Until your children are teens, they will not eat a great deal for lunch. And packing a huge amount of lunch will actually discourage them because it will look like too much to tackle. For your young ones, buy little bananas and small apples—rather than the ones that look like they were grown on steroids—and little tangerines, apricots, and grapes.

Find out exactly when your middle and high school child is going to eat lunch. You might be in for a surprise: In some schools the cafeteria is so small that lunch has to be eaten in multiple shifts, and these can start as early at 10:30 A.M. or as late as 1:30 P.M. If lunch is very early, your kids might not eat much at all, but they will have a great need for a healthy snack grabbed between classes and another right after school. If their lunchtime is very late, you'll have to make sure they have a good breakfast, because the wait for lunch is a long one.

If you use a thermos, take the following precautions:

- Do not use a thermos to transport carbonated beverages. The top could come off with quite a bang after being shaken all morning in a lunchbox.
- If you microwave the contents, put the thermos in the upright position and keep the top off. Make sure that the contents are not too hot before you put the thermos in the lunchbox, especially if your child has an early lunch.
- For cold foods, pre-chill the thermos bottle by filling it with cold water and ice cubes and letting it stand for five minutes. Pour out the water and refill with the cold food.
- Never fill the thermos bottle all the way to the top: Leave about an inch headroom to provide space for the screw top (on good thermos bottles, tops screw in like corks).

If your young child is not eating very much for lunch, consider making muffins in a minimuffin pan. The small size of the muffins will make the project of eating them more manageable. Pack two or three for a lunch.

The healthier chips, such as vegetable chips, usually don't come in convenient single serving sizes. So beat the system: Portion them out and pack them in small resealable bags yourself.

Packing certain items separately might be a good idea. Sometimes a sandwich becomes soggy if it is packed the night before or even that morning, so your child will end up not eating it. You can avoid some of the "soggy" issue by placing a lettuce leaf between the filling and the bread.

However, for some children it's not that simple. They want to make their own sandwiches, from separate ingredients. If you have one of these picky eaters, let him or her help you pack the lunch, so that it is exactly the way he or she likes it. Pack the ingredients separately for quick assembly at school, and there is a greater chance this lunch will actually be eaten.

The next time your family orders take-out food, save the extra packages of salt, pepper, ketchup, and soy sauce. They're great to pack in a lunch.

Learn from restaurants: Wrap plastic forks, spoons, and knives in paper napkins beforehand. Close the napkin bundles with fun stickers and place them in a basket, ready for a month's worth of school lunches.

One parent solved the buy/bring struggle by making lunch money part of her child's allowance package. The choice was to buy lunch at school with the cash, or pack a lunch and keep the money. Whether this strategy will work will depend in large part on your child's temperament, but it might be worth a try. Also, this will only work if you absolutely do not give in and buy them the things they ought to be using their allowance for anyway.

As corny as it is, a Hershey's "kiss" does carry a special little message along with its little burst of chocolate. (Notice, I said "a" kiss, not a whole bag of them!)

Freeze unsweetened applesauce in small tightly closing containers. In the morning you can pack them with the lunch, and they will keep lunch nice and cold. By lunchtime the applesauce will be mostly defrosted. Yum.

Nonfood Ideas to Make Lunch Sweet

Cutting sandwiches into different shapes can make a difference. I will admit that I never went beyond the "cutting on the diagonal" version of this old trick. But some parents buy cookie cutters in various shapes and make dainty little sandwich cutouts for their children. (Yes, you will have considerable leftover pieces of bread, which you can use for croutons, bread pudding, or bread crumbs.)

Include a note in the lunchbox, or cut out a joke or a cartoon strip from the newspaper. Be on the lookout for silly riddles and jokes and sneak those, too, into the lunchbox. Some parents (and children) enjoy this a lot and include word puzzles, anagrams, cryptograms, and puzzles. Buy cheap out of date "joke-a-day" or "new-word-of-the-day" calendars, to have a ready supply. Cherish the years when this simple fun is appreciated. Your child will soon be too sophisticated to want this sweet affection from you, especially in something as exposed to his peers as his lunchbox.

Buy fun napkins, for instance, napkins featuring the kids' current favorite superheroes or cartoon characters. Then include a different one every day to get some variety going.

If you think of assembling school lunches as more of a game than as an annoying task, you'll do better. And, if meeting your children's nutritional needs is a goal you can embrace with love and imagination, you'll succeed for sure.

Childhood Obesity—Solutions to a Worrisome problem

Childhood obesity, now widely recognized as a near-epidemic in America, is not a simple problem and there is no short answer to solve it. But here are some thoughts on simple and obvious things that need to change. Bad school lunches, bought at school or at fast-food outlets nearby, are not the entire source of the childhood obesity problem, yet they are a substantial contributing factor. Healthy school lunches will help put your kids on the right track to avoid obesity. So let's explore the obesity issue. Knowledge is power: The more we know about the problem, the better we can cope with it.

There is a saying that goes, "If you hear hoofbeats, don't think 'zebra'!" Nothing I mention here is revolutionary, all of it is common sense. We have violated some basic health and food principles, and we have to get back on the right track. No fancy theories or expensive medicines are needed.

Prevention Is Always Best

I hope that you are reading this before your child suffers from a serious weight problem. In that case you can use these ideas, in combination with your own, to keep your entire family at a weight that is healthy for each of them. Teach your children early on to make salads, grab a fruit rather than a candy bar, enjoy cooking with whole foods, and think of mealtime as a happy relaxing time. Talk to them about how these healthy foods are helping them to grow tall and strong, how a good diet will keep them healthy not only now but in the future, and how it will give them the energy to live their lives with gusto. Help them to make that connection. Teach them about correct portion sizes, that treats are great but not things to eat all the time, and that sweet foods are not rewards for being "good."

If you do this you will be helping your children to build healthy bodies that will carry them for the rest of their lives; you also will give them character-building lessons that will stay with them forever. You might be forced to make some unpopular decisions, but then it is not your job as a parent to win a popularity contest. It is up to you to do and teach the right thing.

Catch It Early

Gaining weight does not happen overnight, and neither does losing weight. The faster you start changing the patterns that produce the extra weight, the less drastic the remedies will need to be. If you can see your child getting fat, ask your pediatrician for some confirmation. Little kids often have a little extra padding on them, and sometimes kids will gain a few extra pounds just before a growth spurt. So not all weight gain is a cause for alarm.

But if there is a problem, you must act! In the current environment, this is not something children grow out of naturally. You are setting your child up for many potential health problems and psychological damage as well. To be on the safe side, any weight management program for children should be supervised by a physician or other health professional who has specific training in obesity control. Pediatricians do not necessarily have much knowledge about nutrition per se. Remember, too, that nutrition appropriate for children is different from that which is appropriate for adults.

Is It Really Important?

An obese child is more likely to grow up to become an obese adult. Obese adults are at increased risk for many ailments such as high blood pressure, Type II diabetes, coronary heart disease, angina, congestive heart failure, stroke, gallstones, gout, osteoarthritis, obstructive sleep apnea, some types of cancer, bladder control problems, poor female reproductive health, and an assortment of psychological disorders such as depression, distorted body image, eating disorders, and low self-esteem. Eric Schlosser, author of the best-seller *Fast Food Nation,* writes, " . . . overweight people had a much higher rate of premature death. Severely overweight people were four times as likely to die young than people of normal weight. Moderately overweight people were twice as likely to die young."

To be able to protect your child, even a little bit, from this miserably long and fearsome list of woes is a task worthy of your time and effort. If it makes you feel any better, North Americans are not the only ones to wrestle with this problem. In Japan the rate of obesity has doubled among children just as the consumption of fast food has doubled. Europe is also experiencing an obesity epidemic, with England leading the way.

Eat Real Food

Our bodies were designed to eat what nature provides. Period.

No matter how loudly food manufacturers insist that the chemicals they put in our foods are "fine" and are "proven safe," all you have to do is take a walk through a busy shopping mall to look at people and you will know that something is very wrong! Look at what we are up against: artificial colors, artificial flavors, additives, preservatives, genetically modified fruits and vegetables, hormone- and antibiotic-filled meats, artificial sugars, chemically manufactured vitamins, to name a few. All these might possibly be fine in small doses, once in a while, in an otherwise clean and healthy environment, when children are getting lots of exercise, breathing fresh air, and are under minimal stress. But who knows for sure?

Why would you agree to have your kids be the guinea pigs for this chemical roulette experiment? We have no way of knowing how all these things may affect us over, say, a twenty-year period of growing up, and there have been essentially no experiments to see how these food additive chemicals affect us when taken in combination for long periods!

What we do know is that we have absolute proof that what we are eating is *not* working. So, if only to be on the safe side, follow these two simple rules: First, make 95 percent of the food you eat real food. Food grows on trees, in the ground, on the ground, on bushes, and it comes from animals in the form of meat, milk, or eggs. I.e., food is not created in factories. And second, drink lots of clean water. That's it.

Limit Television

Limit watching television, playing video games, and surfing the Internet on the computer. As long as your child is in the grips of commercial television, you will be fighting an uphill battle, and the greatest gift you can give your child is for him or her to be able to think independently and not to be programmed by commercial advertisers.

This change will make a huge impact, for the better, on your whole life. It will give you and your child some time together, so you can talk, hang out, play, dance, fold the laundry, cook together, and tell silly jokes. You will also limit the pro-junk food commercials your child is exposed to.

When you do watch television, make sure you do not behave like couch potatoes, snacking on high calorie foods. About 43 percent of adolescents watch more than two hours of television each day. No wonder their minds are filled with junk food commercials that make them want to snack on junk. Repetition breeds habits.

If you really understand how dangerous it is to expose your child to this endless television brainwashing, you might choose to go a step further. There is absolutely no need for your child to watch programs when they are actually broadcast. Agree on the programs they are allowed to watch, and tape those shows on a system that allows you to record them so you can play them back without commercials. You can also emphasize PBS shows, which don't have commercials to begin with.

While you are at it, you might also want to unplug yourself from all the commercials. If you doubt that you, too, might need a break from exposure to commercial indoctrination, try the following experiment. Walk down a grocery aisle, for instance, where the cookies, chips, and soda are displayed, and see how many tunes you can hum that belong with these products. Sometimes you can even remember a product's former advertising campaign. If you hear a good many of these jingles in your head, you'll have to face up to the truth: Advertisers have taken up permanent residence in your brain and are influencing your decisions! So give your child a good example and do something more productive with your own time. It's a great way to make room in your life for preparing healthier meals and for getting more exercise.

Exercise Portion Control

One of the factors contributing to American children becoming overweight is that portion sizes have increased substantially. We are now not only overfed but often malnourished at the same time! Restaurants can make it look like they are giving you a good value by increasing their portion sizes. The reason for this is that the cost of their food represents only a relatively small part of their expenses.

At home you have different options to help you control your portions: Use smaller plates! A six-ounce steak with a small baked potato and a cup of steamed carrots and broccoli look anemic on a gigantic 12-inch dinner plate but perfectly fine on an 8-inch salad plate. Take a portion size hint from hospitals and airlines: Have you ever noticed that it looks like their food will not fill you up, because it looks so little, but it actually does. You need to reeducate your eyes, and smaller plates will help you gauge portion sizes better and decrease your temptation to overeat.

"New and Improved" May Not Be "Better"

Not only are portions bigger than they used to be, but the formulas of familiar products have also changed. Ovaltine's formula, for instance, has been changed over the years for the American market; it now has more sugar and less barley malt in it than the European version. Read those food labels and make better decisions.

Offer Yummy Treats

Keep healthy snacks on hand and allow your child easy access to them. If your house is full of cookies, chips, candy, and ice cream, it is much harder for your kids to make wise choices. Cut-up fruits, cleaned veggies with dips, healthy homemade muffins and cookies, air-popped popcorn, rice cakes with peanut butter, yogurt fruit shakes, and lots of other snacks are suggested in this book. If they are available and ready to eat, the craving for junk food will diminish.

Managing Picky Eaters

I can give you some advice here, but I cannot guarantee immediate success. I had three picky eaters who eventually grew up to be great cooks and adventurous eaters.

When my eldest daughter, Sarah, was five, she was in a contest at school called the "2-bite club." To get a certificate she had to eat two bites of a new food. The new food she chose to eat two bites of was oatmeal! (We still have the certificate, by the way; this was BIG, I tell you!) She is now twenty-five and cooks and entertains with imagination, so be patient with your little one.

Maybe you can have your very own "2-bite club" at home with a computer-generated certificate that can be signed, presented, and displayed on the refrigerator every time a new food is tried.

My friend Donna introduced me to the "no thank you portion," whereby you can train your child to eat not-so-favorite foods. Basically you make an agreement with your child that he or she will eat a few bites of these foods to try and get used to them, but the child won't have to eat lots of it at any one meal.

You can also decide together what a "default" meal should be. If the kids really don't like a new meal you've made, there should be an agreed-upon set of foods that they can eat instead. A peanut butter sandwich and an apple was what we agreed on in my house. Depending on the situation, you might also decide that if your child chooses not to eat the regular meal, they cannot have any, or perhaps only half a portion, of the dessert that day. Leverage, bribery, call it what you will. But if the scheme leads your kids toward a healthier diet, you're excused.

One thing you should not do with a picky eater is give up right away on introducing him or her to new foods. Tests show that it takes up to eleven exposures to a new food before a child might embrace it.

Also, do not become a short-order cook for your kids (think about what you are teaching your child here when you bend and bend again in his or her direction), and do not allow your child to substitute snacks for any meal. Skipping an occasional meal is not the end of the world (unless your child is terribly underweight or has an eating disorder), and hunger is a great way to learn gratitude for good food.

If your child eats only one food or a very limited range of foods, you might want to talk to your pediatrician about this. Under these circumstances, make sure your child has a good multivitamin every day. To check if the vitamins you are buying are of high quality, go to the independent lab at consumerlab.com and review its evaluations.

Be the Example

What you do will speak a lot louder than your sermons. As a parent you are always setting the example. Everything you do is being watched, and it is up to you to set the positive example and the high standard you would like your kids to emulate. Nobody said that being a parent was easy. If you buy lots of junk food, the message you give to your household is loud and clear: This is what we eat here. If you eat fresh fruit and salads every day, the message is the same: This is what we eat here.

Your kids will pick up on your attitude. If you think that salads are a punishment, they will, too. If you think outdoor games and exercise are boring, the kids will follow suit. If you think that the television must be on all the time, they'll assume that is the way it has to be.

But if you love to eat fresh stuff, to cook, to move, to talk together, to learn, then this is what your kids will learn. This is your life: Make it fun!

Make Mealtime a Social Time

One of the reasons people—little ones or grown-ups—overeat is because they eat in a hurry and do not concentrate on enjoying their meals. If you eat in front of the television, you're distracted from eating per se, and you may well be putting food in your mouth automatically without knowing exactly how much you have eaten. Instead, sit down to eat, turn the television off, have a meal together, and talk with each other. Slow down for a moment, chew your food thoroughly, and don't rush. It takes about twenty minutes for your brain to get the message that you are full, so if you take your time, you are less likely to overeat.

Mealtimes traditionally have also been a good time to instill manners in children. You know the routine, the catechism: Say "please" and "thank you." Eat with your mouth closed. Ask for the food to be passed and don't reach in front of someone. Ask the people in your family how their day was and then give them your full attention. The television can wait; the people you love need you right now.

Educate Your Children and Yourself

There are quite a few excellent children's books that teach the principles of good nutrition. Ask your local librarian to recommend some that are age appropriate, and read these books to and with your child: You will both benefit from the information. See the Resources at the end of this book for starter suggestions.

Talk about the foods you're buying, or not buying, when you take your kids to the supermarket. Talk to them, too, while you cook and eat. ("All the orange in the carrot is the wonderful vitamin A, which helps to make your eyes see better. Thank you Mr. Carrot!") Be sure to start talking to your children about food early. You are up against the insistent, well-thought-out media campaign by the fast-food and processed-food industry, and you had better get your opinion out there while your kids are still listening to you.

"I Am So Proud of You"

Children's self-esteem suffers a great deal when they are overweight, since they are most likely being teased and are comparing themselves negatively with others. Just telling your kids that they are fine will not necessarily make a great impact, because they know you are trying to make them feel good. The only way to build self-esteem is to feel good about a real accomplishment, and what you, as a parent, can do very effectively is to point out your kids' accomplishments and make them count.

"I am so proud of you because . . . " are words we all love to hear, and your child longs for them! Find things to praise your child for, even if you have to begin very small. "Wow, look at you, you did such a great job eating that apple!" will get you much better results than "You think eating that apple is going to make up for all those crackers you ate with it?" "I can really tell you ate a lot more salad today" will make your child want to eat more salad, whereas "Those stupid three bites of salad are not exactly going to make you skinny," may very well backfire. Don't give with one hand just to take away with the other!

Cook with Your Kids

Not only is cooking with your kids fun, it also allows you a golden opportunity to teach them about ingredients and healthy foods.

I loved cooking with my kids and all three have turned out to be fine cooks in their own right. It was my middle daughter Abigail, though, who was the most enthusiastic as a child. She learned early on to bake cakes and cookies, make perfect dinner rolls, and fold in whipped egg whites, which allowed her to make perfect soufflés before she was in high school. Most cooking is really only a little more difficult than making mud pies, but the results are much more delicious.

Make a cookbook for and with your kids that includes their favorite foods. Most published children's cookbooks concentrate on baking cookies and cakes, because the end results are so very satisfying, but if weight is an issue, concentrate on making healthy sandwiches, salads, and soups. There are many excellent kids' cookbooks on the market. Just be sure to find one that does not emphasize sweets.

Get Outside and Move

Move and help your kids to move. Go outside and play hide-and-seek or "duck-duck-goose," jump rope, put on loud rock-and-roll music and dance, ride your bikes together, work in the garden, make a snowman, go sledding, throw a baseball, kick a soccer ball, throw Frisbees, go roller-skating, go swimming, play tag, walk through nature and have a heart-to-heart talk, climb a mountain, jump on a trampoline, go ice-skating, do a Tae Bo exercise video together (and laugh because you both look silly). Praise yourself and praise your child for any and all movement. Organized, competitive sports, with all their costs and scheduling demands, are not the only ways to get lively, healthy exercise.

Let your kid play outside after school, during daylight hours, unless the weather is really bad. Build some outdoor activity into your daily life. Walk to school if you can, and park farther away from buildings and stores. The sad truth is, many schools' physical education programs have been curtailed, or their methods don't really require students to do anything that is aerobic or strength building. And kids are trapped inside their schools almost all day for nine months of the year. Send them out into the yard or down the street to the park. They need it.

People who suffer from SAD (Seasonal Affective Disorder) develop a depression that sets in during the winter when there is limited daylight. With the depression often comes overeating, especially of sugary foods. This points up the terrific importance of daylight. Help your kids to get some every day they can.

What Your Kids Really Want

Every time children are asked what they wish they could have more of they do *not* say donuts and chocolate. The consistent answer is this: More time with and attention from my parents! Preparing nutritious food together and being physically active will not only give you greater health, but you will be nourishing your child's heart and soul as well. Tell me truly: Do you have anything more important to do?

Be Grateful

A lot of kids used to be admonished to clean their plates because of the "poor starving children in India." Since these hungry children live very far away and have no access to the food on the plate, this tactic makes little practical sense. But many children in this country and in countries around the world *do* go hungry and *are* sick because of nutritional deficiencies. In light of that, for us to be gluttons is deeply inappropriate.

Maybe your family can "adopt" a hungry child through one of the reputable child service agencies. Instead of buying nutritiously empty foods, you might decide to put that money toward helping to feed somebody who is really hungry.

In addition to this, you might want to be aware of how much you actually intend to consume. Food is precious, too precious to be casually thrown away. Become aware of how much you will really eat and put that reasonable amount on your plate. Use the leftovers in your next meal. Being grateful for the food you have, and sharing some with somebody who truly needs it, will fill an empty space in you that no fast-food junk meal can possibly satisfy.

Tools and Staples for Healthy School Lunches

Not everyone had a mom or a dad who taught them how to cook, and not everyone loves cooking. So, for those who feel a bit out of their depth in the kitchen, here are some notes about kitchen tools, skills, and food supplies that will help make school lunch prep time more convenient and healthy.

You may well know some of these tricks already. Just grab the ones that look helpful to you and then leap forward. If you are already happy with the way you are doing things, by all means, adapt these ideas to suit your methods!

Baking Cups

These are paper or foil cups that line muffin tins. Baking cups go a long way in helping eliminate the scraping and cleaning up of a muffin pan, a job I totally detest. If you use paper cups and eat the muffins while they are still warm, a lot of the muffin will stick to the paper. However, once the muffins cool, the paper will peel off nicely. The foil baking cups do not stick to the muffin, even while warm. If you like to serve muffins hot, this is the way to go, or consider investing in a high-quality nonstick muffin tin.

You can also spray the muffin tin with a nonstick spray. If you spray the tin thoroughly, your muffins will come out easily, but you will have to wash the tin after cooking a batch.

Food Processor

I use my food processor all the time, and I cannot recommend it highly enough. I have an old one, which has stood up to unbelievable use and abuse, and I consider it the one essential electrical tool in my kitchen. Every other thing I can fake: I can toast bread in a frying pan, I can open a can with a manual can opener, I could just possibly live without my blender (though that is appliance #2), but there are a lot of dishes I could not make without my trusty food processor. It is worth learning how to use the various attachments so you can shred carrots, mix cookie dough, and whip cream with ease and confidence. If you cook a lot, a second bowl is a worthwhile investment.

Blender

There are things the food processor won't do but a blender will. For example, the blender is ideal for making fruit shakes and homemade salad dressings. A quick yogurt and fruit shake is a great snack after coming home from a long day at school. You can mix the ingredients in the blender container, and your slightly older, well-trained child can run the machine. I would keep young kids away from blenders.

Nonstick Cookie Baking Sheets

These are worth their weight in gold since they will save you lots of annoying scrubbing time. Use only plastic utensils on these and all other nonstick surfaces, no matter what the label says.

Staples

Some food supplies to keep on hand include:

Baking Powder

Though the recipes in this book will instruct you to "add baking powder," you are always best off sifting it first to make sure there are no lumps. Finding a lump of baking powder in a muffin is a disgusting experience. When buying baking powder, be sure to get one with no aluminum additives, since this metal, even in trace amounts, has been implicated in Alzheimer's disease.

Baking Soda

Finding a lump of baking soda in your quick bread is just as bad as finding a lump of baking powder, so be sure to sift it, too, before adding it.

Baking soda is activated by a "sour" or acid ingredient in the batter, either buttermilk or vinegar. The "rising action" (which is actually the making of small bubbles) is an immediate, chemical one and starts the moment the two ingredients find each other. If you mix a batter with baking soda too vigorously, you will break the bubbles, and your baked product will be flat. The moment you see baking soda in a recipe, it means that you will need to mix the batter with long efficient strokes, quickly but thoroughly, and not let the mixed batter sit. Pour the batter into the baking pan carefully as soon as it is mixed and bake it right away.

Butter

In all recipes I use sweet (unsalted) butter for a very simple reason: I love the taste of butter, and I distrust margarine. Use your common sense here and read the ingredients on the margarine tub: Your body is not meant to ingest chemicals, it is designed to digest food! Margarine was invented as a cheap, durable butter substitute for the soldiers in Napoleon's army. If you are under strict doctor's orders not to eat butter, then follow the doctor's advice. Otherwise, use butter with moderation and enjoy every little bit of it.

Cultured Buttermilk Blend Powder

I like baked goods made with buttermilk, which is the liquid that is left over after the cream has been skimmed from the whole milk. I seldom needed a full quart of it when cooking, though, so I would resist making the recipes, because I didn't want the rest to go to waste. Dry buttermilk powder is a great solution because it is easy to reconstitute and gives excellent results. If you'd rather use fresh buttermilk in these recipes, by all means substitute the water part in the recipes (which is meant to reconstitute the powder) with fresh buttermilk.

Light Brown Sugar

This is the sugar I use most often in baking, mainly because I find it has more flavor than white sugar. Dark brown sugar has a distinctive molasses taste, which is too overpowering in most baked goods. If your child has a strong reaction to sugar or is diabetic, you'll have to get other cookbooks to help you with suggestions. I have found that "naturally sweet" baking books end up using honey liberally, and that will most likely affect your child in the same way sugar does. Your best bet will be cookbooks geared specifically toward diabetics, which have to avoid the adrenaline spike caused by the sugar. For all of us, kids and adults alike, the best way to handle high-sugar snacks is by making sure we have protein in the same meal, and to make sure the portion is governed by common sense and not desire.

Milk

Throughout these recipes I use 2 percent milk. Feel free to use whole milk or nonfat milk. The results will be slightly different, but none of these recipes is so sensitive that this adjustment will significantly affect the result.

Nuts

When you are cooking for your very young children, you might choose not to add nuts to their foods. Lunchrooms are not quiet places where food is thoughtfully and carefully chewed, and small nut pieces can present a choking hazard. This is the main reason why I have, for the most part, omitted chopped nuts from these recipes.

Olive Oil

For dressings and sautéing I use extra-virgin olive oil, because I like the fruity taste and because it is "heart healthy." For baking I use extra-light-tasting olive oil, because I don't want the taste of olives in my muffins and cakes.

Tahini

Tahini is a paste made from ground sesame seeds and has been used as a food since at least 3000 B.C. Tahini continues to be a delicious and healthful addition to our pantry. It is also very high in calcium, the great natural relaxer of muscles and minds.

Whole Wheat Flour

In most baking recipes I use whole wheat flour. White flour is made by eliminating the very ingredients that make flour good for us: vitamins, minerals, fiber, and all manner of micronutrients. Replacing a few of those nutrients with some chemically produced vitamins cannot compare to the real thing. If you do use white flour, make sure that it is not bleached.

Refrigerate your flour, since the fats in flour can go rancid, and try to buy your flour from a store that has a lot of turnover so that it is as fresh as possible.

What I Don't Use

Microwave Oven

OK, so mine is the last household on the North American continent to hold out, but I do *not* use a microwave. Most people only use it to warm up their coffee anyway, and I like my coffee, when I drink it, through the whole range of temperatures. I am willing to admit that some of my reasons for distrusting and disliking the microwave are irrational, but let me give you a few really good ones.

There are genuine health concerns that have to do with the commercial packaging materials and the plastic that might come in contact with your microwaved food (such as the plastic wrapping). Once these wrappings are heated to extremely high temperatures, which they are in the microwave, they can produce potential cancer-forming substances that can get into the food. Food, too, is chemically altered once it is nuked, and who knows what the long-term effects of that will be. I know, that's a lot of maybes, but I personally don't want to find out in twenty years that microwaving was conclusively proven to be bad for my child, or for me. Do you?

Most people argue that it is the speed with which foods cook in the microwave that they like so much. First of all, one of the experiences you have with conventional cooking is that you can smell the food for a while before you eat it. Not only is this a wonderful experience, I think it is a psychologically necessary part of feeling satisfied. First you handle the raw food (not if it's frozen or a processed substitute), then you smell it while you prepare it and while it is cooking, and only then do you eat it. All of your senses get a chance to participate and the entire experience is satisfying.

If you are still so in love with the idea of speed, let me ask you this: What have you done with all that time you saved? Did you write your novel? Did you use it to hug your kids and tell them how much they mean to you? Did you stuff those envelopes for that charity cause? If so, microwave on. If not, slow down, make better and more efficient use of your time through better planning, and enjoy your food and your family.

Warning: A microwave is not automatically a safe object around small children. Things get heated up to temperatures that can easily scald. Be sure to give your child specific instructions and warnings before you do let her use this appliance. Many children are burned by scalding hot beverages and the superhot steam that is released when opening a package of otherwise innocent popcorn.

Artificial Sweeteners

If you drink diet soda, try the following experiment. Drink a soda without a meal or other snack and notice how you feel fifteen or twenty minutes later. You will almost certainly have a strong craving for something sweet. The reason is simple. Your mouth thought you were eating something sweet and gave your body the signal to make insulin to counteract the spike in blood sugar that would surely follow. But there is no sugar, and now your body finds itself with all this insulin and nothing to use it on. So now you need to get something that has sugar into your system to use the insulin you produced. So you go and buy a candy bar and you negate any advantage you thought you had with the zero-calorie drink!

Artificial sweeteners come and go on the market and are promoted as safe, but how sure can you be that this is really true? In fact, every so often a sweetener that was supposed to be safe is taken off the market because new studies show it to be a health hazard! There is no "artificial sweetener" tree or bush in nature, so how can your body know how to process it? And even if it does pass through your body untouched (as some manufacturers suggest, ignoring what Biology 101 taught you about digestion), it is a foreign substance that does not belong there. How can you know how your body will react? Did your liver, which has to process all these chemicals, assure you that it had excess capacity and could handle it? I cannot imagine that it can possibly be a good thing for a young and growing body, and I hope you will play it safe and not feed artificial sweeteners to your child.

Soda

Each can of soda contains the equivalent of about ten teaspoons of sugar. The typical teenage boy today gets about 9 percent of his daily calories from soft drinks! There are even more serious problems: Excessive soda consumption can lead to calcium deficiencies and a greater likelihood of bone fractures. If you want to make a single change in your child's health, eliminating all sugared and artificially sugared drinks would be a great one.

Water is the best thing to drink, and everybody needs lots of water to remain healthy. After all, it's 70 percent of what we are.

The Roots of the Problem

OK. So, tomorrow's school lunches are already assembled and waiting in the fridge for the morning rush hour when the kids, and maybe you, too, will race out the door. We've had our fun for today cooking with the young ones. Now let's take some time to ponder seriously, as adults, how it is that societies as rich and as smart as those in North America have allowed themselves to develop bad habits in the areas of food and exercise, habits with decidedly unhappy results in terms of overall health for young people. Countries much poorer than ours are feeding their children better than we do.

Think of the irony: Our older people, in their seventies and upwards, are living longer and better than ever. But our kids are beset on all sides with health troubles that can actually shorten their lives. These troubles are often related to food and exercise.

What went wrong? In this section we'll dig deeper into the problem, taking a look at culture and economics. What does this have to do with healthy school lunches? Read on.

Life in the Fast Lane

Life in North America has changed radically in the last hundred years, and it has changed at breakneck speed in the last forty or so years. But our bodies and genetics do not change as quickly, and the rules by which our bodies organize themselves are the same now as they were 3,000 years ago. Our needs for sleep, movement, clean water, wholesome food, unpolluted air, entertainment, and community have not changed, but our society has changed dramatically in the ways it provides for these needs.

No longer do we go to sleep when it is dark and wake up when it gets light again. Instead we can have bright lights around us all day and all night, and we use an alarm clock to wake us before we are done sleeping. Physical movement is no longer needed to attend to basic chores, such as hunting animals, tending the fields, chopping wood, or kneading bread.

We now drive to work, buy our food already prepared, and sit all night, isolated in our own little house, watching our entertainment pour forth from little boxes called televisions and computer terminals.

Our water has a different pH level now than it did 3,000 years ago; our vegetables have foreign genes injected or designed into them; and we eat massive quantities of foods that nature did not produce. No wonder our bodies are in revolt! The assault on our bodies is so extensive that the damage is no longer waiting to reveal itself until middle- or old age, but is manifesting itself in our children.

I know that there is a lot of controversy out there about food, diet, and health. You will have no problem finding "authorities" who will argue long and loud that whatever they are doing to the food and water is not the problem. Some tell you fat is the problem. Others shout at you that we are poisoning ourselves with too much protein. "Experts" tell you that microwaving is completely safe; that an "enriched" product is the equivalent of, or superior to, the original natural product; that synthetic vitamins are of the same quality as the ones found in food; that the minute quantities of artificial color, artificial flavor, and preservatives added to food could not possibly matter; and that frozen foods have the same nutritional value as fresh.

But wait. Look around you and ask yourself: How is it going for your kids and their friends? We raised these children in a world that has been safer and more abundant than almost any place or time in history, and yet our kids are having problems staying lean, feeling energetic and lively, behaving properly, learning easily, and believing that they should be robustly optimistic about their lives!

There is no easy answer to this flux of problems, there is no one single thing that went wrong, but the disaster created by the combination of all these factors is most visible in the fact that American children are getting obese at alarming rates.

Is There a Real Problem?

With all the media hype that surrounds us, it is often hard to tell the real issues from the trumped-up ones designed to boost television ratings. So is there really a health crisis that concerns our children?

Five years ago, 11.3 percent of those ages six to eleven and 10.5 percent of those ages twelve to nineteen were considered overweight. Certainly these are figures that should have concerned us. However, the 2003 update of the American Heart Association's "Heart Disease and

Stroke Statistics" reports now that more than 15 percent of children and adolescents ages six to nineteen are considered overweight or obese, and that translates into nine million children. Even toddlers are affected: 10 percent of children between the ages of two and five suffer from being seriously overweight. The dramatic increase in these numbers is why childhood obesity in this country is considered an epidemic.

Dr. D. M. Styne, M.D., of the Department of Pediatrics at the University of California Medical Center, Davis, reports, "We and others have seen children between the ages of six through ten years with a BMI (Body Mass Index) over the 99th percentile who die of sudden cardiopulmonary arrest apparently caused by arrhythmias associated with their obesity." Translated, this means that obese children are having heart attacks!

Overall, America ranks a distressing number twenty-four in healthy life expectancy in the world! So the short answer is yes, there is a real problem and yes, you should be concerned.

What Is Normal Weight, Anyway?

Body Mass Index (BMI) for both adults and children is currently a popular tool with which health professionals determine if a person is overweight, underweight, or just right. It is based on a formula that takes into account only the weight and height of a person.

A BMI "growth chart" is used to help assess whether a child or adolescent is overweight. Exercise professionals in particular do not like the BMI because it allows neither leeway for athletes who have a great deal of muscle (which is heavy) nor adjustment of "proper weight" for those who are built with slight frames. A competent physician will consider not only your children's BMI numbers, but also their build and growth patterns to determine whether their weights are healthy.

What's Up with the Food?

Why are our children not eating wholesome foods in appropriate amounts? A good part of the reason for this is because they have been "programmed" by commercials on television to expect cereals that come in bright colors and dinners that come in a box with a toy.

Let me give you an example. A young friend of mine works with autistic toddlers between the ages of two and five. Stephanie is one of the lucky people in this world who has found work she loves. She hates seeing the children leave at the end of the day and when she wakes up in the morning she can't wait to see "her" kids again. I asked her if they gave the children in this program a special diet to help support and heal their neurological problems. Stephanie made a face and told me that would be almost impossible. "We ran an experiment," she said. "One week we had plain old hamburgers and fries, and they hardly touched it. The next week we had the same meal, but we had collected containers from a fast-food place, and we put the burgers and fries in those containers and bags and presented that lunch to them. The food was exactly the same as the previous week, but this time they ate it all."

If you really want to understand how fast food has changed the way Americans, and increasingly other peoples as well, eat and think about food, read *Fast Food Nation* by Eric Schlosser. Study Schlosser like you did your texts in school, and mark it up with a highlighter, lest you forget the most important points. His analysis is worth your time.

Your children have been consciously, deliberately, and cynically sold fast food since they were tots. Corporations know that young children can often recognize a logo before they recognize their own name in print, and they make sure that the company logo is in your kids' faces from the moment they enter the marketplace as consumers, and that means from the day you turn on the television.

You might be surprised at how good your child seems at getting you to bring him to a fast-food restaurant. This is not an accident. The power of children to persuade has been thoroughly studied, and you should feel fortunate that your kids are not reading up to make themselves even better at it. There are, according to McNeal, in his book *Kids as Customers*, seven major categories of nagging, though children will stick with the one or two that are most effective. Advertisers know you and your children better than you know yourself, and children know exactly how to push your buttons. As the adult, and the person in charge of their health, both now and long-term, you must educate yourself and your children, and you have to make them aware of the fact that they are being "sold."

Your only defense is lots and lots of prevention, education, and modeling. Limiting your child's television viewing time has the double benefit of making more time for them to exercise and less time for them to be indoctrinated. The typical American child now watches twenty-one hours of television per week, and that does not include all the time they sit in front of other screens. During the course of a year they watch more than 30,000 television commercials, and, in total, the fast-food industry spends about three billion dollars annually to promote its food. No wonder our kids want it. They have been thoroughly brainwashed!

But now the fast-food companies and major food manufacturers are under siege. Some are being sued in class action suits modeled on the successful class action lawsuits brought against tobacco companies. It's beginning to look like some of the big guns will make some changes. But even if they do, they are still not on your side by a long shot. Look at the nutritional information posted on the Web sites of your favorite fast-food places. I think you'll be surprised at what you find. The difference between a small order of French fries and a supersized one—on the McDonald's Web site—is a difference of 400 calories. Look at its Caesar Salad (without chicken) and you'll find that the salad is a very reasonable 90 calories, but you get hit with 190 calories in the creamy dressing. (A word of warning: Salad dressing packages often contain more than one serving, but the calories are given to you per serving. Pretty tricky, right?) Burger King chooses to give you the calories of its sandwiches with and without the mayo; a 160 calorie difference right there to consider!

Some single foods are also terribly high in calories by themselves. A thirty-two-ounce vanilla shake has 1,140 calories. And, of course, size matters: A twelve-ounce soft drink contains about 110 calories, but the forty-two-ounce "supersize" contains 410 calories!

The confusion and deception in the industry is deep and wide, and your only defense is your willingness to educate and be educated.

The School Cafeteria Dilemma

Fast food can now also be found in the school cafeteria, making it tempting for your child to eat popular but fattening meals instead of healthy lunches.

Fast food has managed to invade the schools in the most pernicious of ways. Giant fast-food corporations or their local outlets promise the school money, which it desperately needs for all sorts of programs that are underfunded or cut back and which would actually benefit the children. Profit sharing on soda machines is one way they do it. After many years of clever advertising by the fast-food companies, fast food and soda are more appealing to a child than is "regular" food, and having it close by and so convenient would pose, even for the most saintly of kids, a terrific temptation. In one Midwest school the principal actually told the teachers to "push" the soft drink sales in order to meet the school's financial goals! There are textbook publishers and manufacturers of school notebooks and tote bags that have succumbed to placing fast-food companies' logos on their products so that even in the classroom itself there is no escaping the insistent reinforcement of the same message: Buy our product.

Irradiated Food in School

Before you allow your child to eat in the school cafeteria, you might want to investigate it a little. A bill passed in May 2002 directs the Agriculture Department to buy irradiated beef for the federal school lunch program. Local school boards will make up their minds if they want it, and you might just want to know what your local board has decided. The reason for the irradiation, we are told, is to kill contaminants. Contaminants can be, and currently are, checked for by other long-established testing methods, but irradiation, they say, will allow for "sanitized" food in our schools. Irradiation as a substitute for testing? The objection many people have, on a gut level, is that they fear that some "radiation" might be left behind in the food. That is actually not the case. What *is* true is that radiation alters molecules (otherwise it could not "kill" anything), and we have no idea what the long-term effects of these altered molecules on our children will be.

There is now a lobbying effort that would allow schools serving irradiated meat to call it instead "pasteurized" food rather than "irradiated." Louis Pasteur was a good guy, right? So how could irradiated food be bad? Slippery logic at best, blatant obfuscation at worst. So, as a parent, beware of what you are told!

No Exercise

Children, especially girls, become less active as they move through adolescence. Physical inactivity is more prevalent among women than men, and among blacks and Hispanics more so than among whites. For example, the data show that by age fifteen or sixteen, 56 percent of black girls say they are physically inactive during leisure time. About 31 percent of white girls say they are physically inactive.

Just over half of high school students were enrolled in physical education classes in 2001. However, only a third attended physical education classes daily. We need daily exercise. People who are inactive are 1.5 to 2.4 times more likely to develop heart disease. A good lunch for your kids is important, but it could lose its effectiveness if children are allowed to develop a sedentary lifestyle.

The Risks Your Child Runs

In the past most people considered a child's weight to be primarily a cosmetic issue. The fat kid in the class was picked on and it "hurt his or her feelings." In fact, the most immediate consequence of being overweight as perceived by the children themselves is social discrimination, which is associated with poor self-esteem and depression.

As sad as that is, and even though it really does need to be dealt with, that is right now not necessarily the most pressing physical problem. Children are running serious health risks, risks that threaten their lives right now and risks that will carry over into adulthood and set them up for a life of infirmity and premature death. The most widely recognized and well-studied health risks obese children run are heart disease and diabetes and the far greater risk of becoming an obese adult.

Heart Disease

Risk factors for heart disease, such as high cholesterol and high blood pressure, occur with increased frequency in overweight children and adolescents compared to children of a healthy weight. Two related studies by a pediatric cardiologist at the Children's Hospital Medical Center in Cincinnati, Ohio, suggest that obesity in children directly affects the structure and function of the heart and may increase the risk for heart disease for obese children. One of the studies shows that the size of one of the heart muscles appears to increase in obese children and has been linked to a variety of health problems, including irregular heart rhythms and, in older adults, atrial fibrillation and stroke. In addition, the study uncovered significant abnormalities in heart function.

Diabetes

A study by researchers at Yale University has found that 25 percent of overweight or obese children ages four to ten were showing signs of "insulin resistance." The researchers also found that in the eleven to eighteen age group, 21 percent had signs of insulin resistance. Considering the fact that insulin resistance is typically present but unknown for about a decade before Type II diabetes is diagnosed, obese children could be confronting this disease very soon. A quarter of obese children are already showing signs of changes that could lead to full-blown diabetes. Associate Professor of Endocrinology Sonia Caprio, who led the study, said: "Most of the children are at high risk for Type II diabetes." She continues, "And, if they develop diabetes before the age of 20, they face a lifetime of being at very high risk for complications." However, she said that there was no reason to suppose that the damaging changes already happening in preteen children could not be reversed if they began to lose weight. Type II diabetes, previously considered an adult disease, has increased dramatically in children and adolescents.

Last year, the *New England Journal of Medicine* proclaimed that in fact one can "cure" Type II diabetes with diet and exercise.

Adult Obesity

Overweight adolescents have a 70 percent chance of becoming overweight or obese adults. This increases to 80 percent if one or more parent is overweight or obese. Overweight or obese adults are at risk for a number of health problems including heart disease, Type II diabetes, high blood pressure, and some forms of cancer.

If you're overweight by age five, you've got an 80 percent risk of being overweight as an adult and are susceptible to illnesses such as heart disease. Three out of four children who are obese at age twelve will be obese as an adult.

In Conclusion

It is now thought that the estimated annual cost of treating obesity-related diseases is about $100 billion. About $127 million per year is spent treating overweight children. But how much is even one life, your child's life, worth?

A number of factors have combined to make the obesity in children trend happen so quickly, and it will take a number of adjustments on a number of different fronts to make a significant change. We, the adults in charge of their lives, must make changes. We don't need to wait for a new diet drug or more information from better and larger studies to prevent this suffering. We can't wait for slow-moving legislation to make a difference, and the fast-food companies cannot be trusted to make the sorts of changes that would significantly reduce the problem. They serve the financial interests of their stockholders, not the health interests of your children. We can't wait to see if the lawsuits pending against the fast-food companies will bring about meaningful change.

The power to improve this unhappy situation is entirely in our own hands, and we as consumers are the only ones who can make a big difference, and make it soon. We'll have to alter the way we buy, eat, and prepare food. We have to reform the way we talk to our children about food and what we'll permit in our houses. We'll have to persuade school boards and their cafeteria managers to take this health situation seriously and start serving healthier foods and to forbid fast food and sugary drinks to be served. We have to make sure—even if the schools do not—that there is time and opportunity for our kids to exercise regularly.

As adults who love our children, we have to make childhood obesity an important enough issue so that we are willing to make the necessary changes. Preparing wholesome, whole food lunches, with the cooperation of your child, is a great step you can take right now to improve his or her daily life and life expectancy. It's fun, it's easy, and you'll be making a huge, positive contribution to your child's healthy future.

Healthy,
Delicious Lunches
Kids Will Love

Sandwiches

Sandwiches are always the centerpiece of brown-bag lunches, so it is really important that your child will eat what you make and not barter it away. This section presents a wide array of sandwich options.

Together with your child, make a list of all the breads, spreads, and toppings he or she likes and you approve of. If your child comes up with a lot of unhealthy choices, make a bargain. Let the burgers, hotdogs, fries, and sodas be limited to one day a week, for instance. Reward this decision with nonfood treats, such as a video rental, an afternoon at the park or beach, or some new socks.

Making a lot of sandwiches is easier if you do it assembly-line style, a fun thing to do even with a fairly young child. Line up the slices of bread on the counter and spread them with butter, mayonnaise, or mustard; then put the filling on the bottom slices and top them off with the remaining pieces of bread. If you want to be really efficient, make extra sandwiches and freeze them. The first chapter lists items that will and won't freeze well. If you are using soft bread, you can freeze the slices before you assemble them so that they won't rip when you spread on hard butter or peanut butter.

It is usually in the lunchtime sandwich that your child will get the protein he or she needs for the sustained energy required by a long afternoon. Eating just carbohydrates for lunch might make his or her energy spike and then dip so low that by late afternoon he or she will look for a sugary snack to compensate. If you are making a sandwich without meat, cheese, or egg, look for a different way to pack up some protein. Beans, for instance in a bean dip, have protein, which you can add to the lunch as a dip with some veggies. Maybe you can toss some hard-boiled egg into a salad or include string cheese or a chunk of cheddar as a snack.

Try to make most of the sandwiches from whole, unadulterated foods that contain no preservatives, artificial dyes and flavors, MSG, and so forth. Choose turkey breast rather than salami (which contains all sorts of added chemicals), natural cheese rather than processed cheese, whole wheat and sprouted wheat bread rather than white bread, all fruit spread instead of jams and jellies that contain added sugar. If your child is overweight, you should consider using reduced-fat dairy products, but the strategy might backfire. First of all, your growing child needs fats for his or her health, and second, nonfat or reduced fat products don't taste as good, and your child might not eat the homemade lunch at all and opt for junk food instead.

The Mighty Meat Sandwich

For most kids most of the time, a meat sandwich will be the one you'll end up making. The way to keep these sandwiches exciting is to vary the bread, the spread, the proteins, and the vegetable garnish. Keep different kinds of sliced bread and rolls in the freezer so that you don't waste food. Portion control is key and your child's age, size, and appetite will have to guide you. Shop carefully to limit the amount of processed meat products you feed your kids. Processed meats (bologna and its many cousins) have all sorts of questionable additives and preservatives in them. Stick with "real" meat such as roast beef, ham, and sliced turkey breast, and go easy on the salami sandwiches.

Breads to Try

Good sandwich bread choices include whole wheat, rye, whole wheat bagels, focaccia, rice cakes, whole wheat crackers, whole grain wraps, whole grain waffles, whole wheat raisin bread, whole wheat cinnamon bread, and flour tortillas. Less nutritious choices are white bread, hard rolls, hotdog rolls, croissants, graham crackers, and English muffins. Use these only occasionally.

BLT

This classic sandwich can be made with some vegetarian and lower-in-fat substitutes. Smoked tempeh is a soybean product available at most supermarkets, and it is much lower in fat than bacon. Be sure to get the smoked tempeh; plain tempeh has very little flavor. You can also make this sandwich with a few bacon bits. Makes 1 sandwich.

2 slices bread, toasted if you like
Mayonnaise
2 lettuce leaves
½ tomato, sliced
4 smoked tempeh strips or other bacon substitute

Spread the mayonnaise on the two slices of bread. On one slice place a lettuce leaf, the tomato slices, and the tempeh. Top that with the other slice of lettuce and the remaining piece of bread. Cut into triangles and wrap tightly in plastic wrap.

Variations

- If you are a purist, by all means use the bacon strips instead.
- Try thinly sliced smoked tofu instead of the tempeh.

Egg Salad Sandwich

Check to see if your supermarket carries organic eggs, which are delicious and provide superior nutrition for you and your child. If you make egg salad yourself, you can control the amount of fat in this salad very easily. For example, you can use only yogurt as a dressing, since the creamy texture comes in good part from the mashed egg yolks. For an older child, you will certainly want to use two eggs. Mashing an egg is an easy task even a very young child can do. Unless your children's doctor advises you to do so, don't omit the egg yolk from this salad. It won't taste as good and the yolk of a good quality egg provides many vital nutrients. Makes 1 sandwich.

1 egg, hard-boiled and peeled
½ teaspoon nonfat yogurt
½ teaspoon mayonnaise
Salt and pepper
2 lettuce leaves
2 slices of bread, toasted

1. Place the egg, yogurt, and mayonnaise in a bowl, mash, and mix thoroughly. Add salt and pepper to taste.
2. Make the sandwich by placing a lettuce leaf on the bread, then the egg salad, then the second lettuce leaf, and the second piece of bread on top. Wrap tightly in plastic wrap.

HARD-BOILING EGGS

The easiest way to hard-boil eggs is as follows: Place eggs in a medium saucepan and cover them with cold water by an inch. Over medium heat bring the water to a boil. When the water has come to a boil, take the pan off the heat, cover it, and let it sit for 12 minutes (set a timer).

Run cold water over the eggs so that the cooking process is stopped. Cool the eggs and refrigerate for up to 3 days.

Meat Sandwich Varieties

In addition to the sandwiches described in this chapter, here are some more winning combinations:

- **Sliced chicken breast, Swiss cheese, caramelized onions**
- **Sliced chicken breast, lettuce, tomato, buttermilk dressing**
- **Sliced chicken breast, shredded lettuce, shredded carrots peanut dressing**
- **Sliced turkey breast, lettuce, cranberry sauce**
- **Sliced turkey breast, lettuce, red pepper strips, blue cheese dip**
- **Sliced smoked turkey breast, sharp cheddar, roasted red peppers, mayo-mustard spread**
- **Sliced roast beef, lettuce, tomato, bacon, Russian dressing**
- **Sliced roast beef, cheddar cheese, tomato, mayonnaise**
- **Sliced roast beef, roasted vegetables**
- **Sliced ham, Swiss cheese, tomato, buttermilk dressing**
- **Sliced ham, lettuce, pineapple ring, mayonnaise**
- **Sliced salami, pickles, mustard**
- **Sliced salami, provolone cheese, carmelized onions**

Instead of making "flat" sandwiches, try making wraps. It makes for an updated presentation, which is currently very popular. It also allows you to fold in some vegetables, which might otherwise be left out of a flat sandwich. Different breads for making wraps are available in the supermarket. You can also cut a pita bread in half horizontally, so that you have two flat rounds, which you can use for making small wraps. Always wrap this sandwich tightly in plastic wrap to keep the contents from falling out.

Tuna Salad Sandwich

This is one of the reliable old standbys. The trick to making this a delicious experience is to line the slices of bread or the pita pocket with lettuce leaves so the bread does not get soggy. You can jazz it up, too, by adding little bits of minced crunchy vegetables. If you use oil-packed tuna, save the oil and use it to make a delicious "fishy tasting" vinaigrette for a salad. Makes 1 sandwich.

2 slices of bread or 1 pita pocket cut open at the top
2 lettuce leaves
3 ounces canned water-packed tuna, drained well
2 teaspoons mayonnaise
2 teaspoons low-fat yogurt
1 tablespoon minced celery
1 tablespoon minced carrot
Salt and pepper

1. Place clean and very dry lettuce leaves on the pieces of bread or in a pita pocket.
2. In a bowl mix the tuna, mayonnaise, and yogurt. Add the celery, carrot, salt, and pepper and mix again.
3. Place the salad on the lettuce leaves and put one slice of bread on the other, lettuce side down, or carefully scoop the salad into the pita pocket, inside the lettuce leaves. Wrap tightly in plastic wrap.

Salmon Salad Sandwich

Salmon salad might be the fish salad your child likes before she gets used to tuna fish salad, since salmon has such a mild taste. This is very easy to make right after you have poached salmon for dinner, but of course you can make it with canned salmon. Makes 1 sandwich.

½ cup poached salmon or canned salmon, drained
2 teaspoons nonfat yogurt
2 teaspoons mayonnaise
1 tablespoon minced scallions (optional)
Salt and pepper
2 slices whole wheat bread or 1 whole wheat pita pocket cut open at the top

1. Place the salmon, yogurt, mayonnaise, and scallions in a bowl and mix well. Add salt and pepper to taste. Chill.
2. Make a sandwich or fill the pita pocket. Wrap tightly in plastic wrap. Pack it very cold, and add an ice pack to the lunchbox.

Savory Spreads

Mayo-Mustard Spread

This super easy spread is a perennial favorite with most lunch meats and cheeses. Make it once a week and it will be ready for you when you need it. Even a very small child can mix this up with a spoon in a plastic jar. Makes ½ cup.

¼ cup mayonnaise
¼ cup yogurt
1 teaspoon to 1 tablespoon Dijon mustard (this depends on personal preference)

Mix ingredients thoroughly and refrigerate in an airtight container.

Russian Dressing

This is a super easy dressing for a very young cook to make. Mixing the two ingredients with a spoon is a satisfying artistic project: First the pale yellow mayonnaise, the white yogurt, and the red ketchup make swirls and then they just make one rosy color. It is a favorite spread on sandwiches and a delicious dip with cut-up vegetables. Makes ¾ cup.

¼ cup mayonnaise
¼ cup yogurt
¼ cup tomato ketchup

Mix ingredients thoroughly in a bowl and chill in an airtight container.

Honey Butter

Make your own honey butter in just a few minutes. Even a young child can easily mash the two ingredients together to make this treat. Makes ¾ cup.

½ cup butter, at room temperature
¼ cup honey

Cream together the butter and honey. Store in the refrigerator. Bring to room temperature before spreading.

Variations

To the honey mixture add any of the following and blend well:

- A sprinkle of cloves and mace
- A sprinkle of cinnamon and nutmeg
- A few drops of vanilla extract and some raisins
- A few drops of orange extract and some cut-up apricots
- One tablespoon grated carrots
- One tablespoon finely chopped walnuts
- One tablespoon grated unsweetened coconut

Bagel with Tomato and Scallion Cream Cheese

You can buy flavored cream cheese for variety. But you can also make your own in a few minutes, and then you can be sure it's fresh and free of preservatives. Use reduced-fat cream cheese if calories are a concern. Makes 1 bagel sandwich.

To make scallion cream cheese

2 ounces cream cheese
1 teaspoon finely minced scallion
Scant ½ teaspoon tamari or soy sauce

Place all ingredients in a shallow bowl and mix well.

To make the sandwich

1 bagel
Scallion cream cheese
2 slices tomato

Cut the bagel in half. Spread the flavored cream cheese on both halves. Top one half with tomato and place the remaining half on top. Wrap tightly in plastic wrap.

Peanut Butter Ideas

My children ate whole wheat bread with peanut butter more often than anything else.

Peanut butter and grape jelly is the American standard, but there are, in fact, lots of variations on this theme. Many different kinds of all-fruit spreads are available that won't add lots of extra sugar. And peanuts are not the only nuts that can be ground. Here are some suggestions:

- **Peanut butter and all-fruit spread**
- **Peanut butter and banana (the second-most eaten sandwich in my house)**
- **Peanut butter, banana, and grated coconut**
- **Peanut butter and pineapple slice**
- **Peanut butter and apple butter**
- **Peanut butter and raisins**
- **Peanut butter and shredded coconut**
- **Almond butter and all-fruit peach spread**
- **Almond butter and apple slices**
- **Almond butter and grated carrot**
- **Cashew butter and all-fruit apricot spread**
- **Cashew butter and pear slices**
- **Cashew butter and dried cranberries**

For a special treat, make a graham cracker peanut butter and banana sandwich.

Bagel with Raisins and Walnut Cream Cheese

If you are making this for a very young child, you'll have to decide if putting the walnuts in the cream cheese is appropriate. Makes 1 bagel sandwich.

To make the walnut cream cheese

2 ounces cream cheese
1½ teaspoon honey
⅛ teaspoon cinnamon
1 tablespoon finely chopped walnuts

Put the cream cheese, honey, and cinnamon in a shallow bowl and mix with a fork. Add the walnuts and blend well.

To make the sandwich

1 bagel
Walnut cream cheese
1 teaspoon raisins

Cut the bagel in half. Spread the flavored cream cheese on both halves. Sprinkle the bottom half with raisins and place the remaining half on top. Wrap tightly in plastic wrap.

Variations

- Instead of raisins try adding a little cut-up dried fruit such as dried peaches, dried cranberries, or prunes.
- Instead of walnuts try adding other nuts such as hazelnuts or pecans.

Bagel and Pineapple Cream Cheese

This is a very pretty cream cheese, and all the little flecks of red and the shredded carrot add some fiber and vitamins. Makes 1 bagel sandwich.

To make the pineapple cream cheese

2 ounces cream cheese
1 tablespoon crushed pineapple, well drained
1 tablespoon finely minced red pepper

Place the cream cheese, pineapple, and red pepper in a shallow bowl and mix well with a fork.

To make the sandwich

1 bagel
Pineapple cream cheese
2 tablespoons shredded carrot

Cut the bagel in half. Spread the flavored cream cheese on both halves. Arrange the shredded carrot on the bottom half and place the remaining half on top. Wrap tightly in plastic wrap.

Variation

- Instead of shredded carrot, substitute a slice of drained canned pineapple.

Cheese and Egg Ideas

Kids like cheese sandwiches, but try adding a vegetable for some extra nutrition. Even if your children do not like sharp cheeses, they might like a mild cheese like goat cheese. (String cheese makes a great snack, too. Pair it up with some miniature carrots and whole wheat crackers.) Here are some ideas:

- Mild cheddar cheese, tomato, lettuce, and mild mustard
- Sharp cheddar cheese and pineapple preserves
- Monterey Jack and green pepper sticks
- Feta cheese, lettuce, tomato, and very thinly sliced red onion
- Goat cheese and roasted vegetables
- Thin slices of mozzarella and tomato slices
- Sliced hard-boiled egg and mayonnaise
- Sliced hard-boiled egg, lettuce, tomato, and a spread made of equal parts of mayonnaise and ketchup

Avocado and Sprouts Science Experiment Sandwich

Make these with your children when they are young; both the avocado and the sprouts provide excellent quality vegetable protein. If the sprouts are homegrown and the avocado pit is sprouted to make a new plant (suspend the pit on toothpicks, bottom end in a glass of water, on the windowsill, and wait patiently for a few weeks), you've provided an entire science curriculum with the lunch as well. Give the avocado a sprinkle of lemon juice to keep it from discoloring to a disappointing, but perfectly edible, brown. Makes 1 sandwich.

2 slices whole grain bread
Mayonnaise or Russian dressing
Avocado slices sprinkled with lemon juice
Sprouts

Make a sandwich in the usual manner. Wrap tightly in plastic wrap.

Tahini, Honey, and Banana Sandwich

Tahini is made from sesame seeds, which are very high in calcium, so this sweet spread packs a respectable nutritional punch as well. Makes 1 sandwich.

1 to 2 tablespoons tahini
1 tablespoon honey
2 slices whole grain bread
Banana slices

1. Mix tahini and honey together.
2. Spread tahini and honey mix on two slices of whole grain bread. Arrange banana slices on one piece of bread and top with the other piece of bread. (If you are making this sandwich at home and want to give your child a real treat, grill the banana sandwich lightly in butter.)

Hummus

What a delicious, all-purpose, good-for-you spread and dip this is! The beans provide some good quality, non-animal, low-fat protein. It's fast, too, taking fewer than 5 minutes to whip up a batch.

For younger children you will probably want to start with one small clove of garlic. How much of the reserved liquid you will add to get the desired consistency will depend on how well you drained the beans to begin with. Makes 1½ cups.

1 15-ounce can garbanzo beans
¼ cup tahini
2 tablespoons lemon juice
1 clove garlic, crushed through a garlic press
Scant ⅛ teaspoon of salt, or to taste
Reserved garbanzo bean liquid, to taste

1. Drain the garbanzo beans, but reserve the liquid.
2. Place the beans, tahini, lemon juice, garlic, and salt in a food processor fitted with the steel blade. Process until smooth. Scrape down the sides.
3. Add the reserved garbanzo bean liquid 1 tablespoon at a time, processing after each addition, until you obtain a spreadlike consistency.
4. Serve with pita bread or as a dip with cut up vegetables such as miniature carrot or celery sticks.

Refried Bean Sandwich Spread

Making Mexican-inspired foods at home lets you monitor the quality of the ingredients, making them much lower in fat than are the fast-food versions. Cooking beans is a very easy process, though it takes a little time, and cooked beans freeze really well, so I highly recommend that you do that. But canned beans work just as well for this recipe. Even small children can help to mash the beans with a fork. Makes about 1 cup.

1 cup cooked beans, pinto or black
½ teaspoon ground cumin
¼ teaspoon salt
Olive oil
Chopped cucumber
Shredded lettuce
Chopped tomato
Salsa
Shredded cheese
Wrapper of your choice

1. In a bowl mash the beans, cumin, and salt.
2. Heat the oil in a skillet and fry the bean mixture until it is dry and solid.
3. Let the mixture cool and store in a closed container in the refrigerator until you are ready to use it.
4. Roll the refried beans with some chopped cucumber, shredded lettuce, chopped tomato, salsa, and shredded cheese in a wrapper.
5. Wrap tightly in plastic wrap.

Pizza to Go

This just might be a "for kids only" idea, since "cold pizza" is not really an acceptable lunch for most people (past college age, that is). Most kids, however, will eat anything that even remotely resembles pizza, so this is worth a try. An older child who has access to a microwave can, of course, heat up this sandwich. Serves 1 to 2.

Pizza to Go Quesadilla Style

2 flour tortillas

¼ cup tomato sauce or pizza sauce

¼ cup shredded cheddar cheese

1. Place one tortilla in the bottom of a nonstick skillet. Turn the heat on to low.
2. Spoon the tomato or pizza sauce on the tortilla and spread it out evenly. Sprinkle the cheese evenly over the sauce. Top with the second tortilla. Cook on both sides, like a grilled cheese sandwich.
3. Place the sandwich on a plate and let it cool. Cut it into wedges.
4. Wrap tightly in plastic wrap.

Pizza to Go French-Bread Style

Make a pizza out of French bread, which you've covered with pizza sauce and topped with shredded cheese. Bake it in the oven until the cheese melts, cool it, and wrap it up.

Variation

- You can top the cheese with small quantities of vegetables and meat.

Calzones

The instructions for calzones have a "do this exactly" part and an improvisation part. The filling, size, and shape of these are completely up to you. I don't think I have ever made one that looked remotely as pretty as any of the illustrations I have seen, or any of the ones I have eaten in restaurants. I just happened to find pizza dough tough to work with, and you might, too. But that has not stopped me, and it shouldn't stop you either, because this is something children and adults alike love.

You can experiment with all sorts of fillings. Putting tomato sauce as one of the ingredients in a dish will make any kid immediately think "pizza," and that gives you a perfect opportunity to sneak in a few tablespoons of vegetables. If you chop them finely, or grate them, your kid might never even know they're there.

The only two things you must pay attention to when making calzones are these: First, wet the seams of the dough before pressing them together; otherwise you will have an imperfect seal and your filling with melt and run out. Second, put the pizza dough into a hot oven, or it won't come out right.

This tastes great hot out of the oven (though you want it to cool for a few minutes, since the filling will be very hot), but it is also good at room temperature the next day. Makes 6 calzones.

1-pound package frozen pizza dough, defrosted
2 to 4 cups filling (recipes follow)
2 teaspoons vegetable oil

1. Preheat the oven to 450° F. This is not optional. You really must preheat the oven if you want pizza dough to come out nice and crisp. Then cover a baking sheet with aluminum foil.
2. Cut the dough into 6 pieces with a sharp, serrated knife. On a floured board roll out each of the pieces to a 6-inch circle.
3. Place a sixth of the filling in the center of the circle. Wet the edges of the dough with water and fold it over to make a half-moon shape. Pinch the edges carefully to seal them.
4. Brush the oil over the tops of the calzones and place them on the baking sheet.

5. Put the calzones in the oven and turn the heat down to 375° F. Bake the calzones for about 25 minutes.

Serve hot or at room temperature.

Calzone Fillings

1 cup shredded mozzarella
¾ cup marinara sauce
1 cup diced green pepper

3 cups Roasted Vegetables (recipe follows)
1 cup crumbled blue cheese or shredded cheddar cheese

4 ounces smoked turkey, sliced
2 cups chopped tomato
1 teaspoon dried oregano
1 cup shredded cheddar

Roasted Vegetables

Roasted vegetables are a great dinner dish, with a perfect lunch follow-up. Many kids will eat their vegetables roasted when they will not eat them steamed or raw. Though I am giving specific vegetables suggestions here, lots of variations are possible. If you make this for dinner, you can also add some potatoes.

Makes 3 cups (depending on the size of the vegetables).

1 small zucchini, cut into 1-inch chunks
1 carrot, cut into ½-inch slices
1 tomato, cut into 6 wedges
1 green pepper, cored and cut into ¾-inch chunks
1 medium onion, cut into ½-inch chunks
¼ cup oil
1 teaspoon salt
1½ teaspoons dried oregano
1½ teaspoons dried basil

1. Preheat the oven to 375° F.
2. In a large bowl combine the zucchini, carrot, tomato, green pepper, onion, and oil. Mix well with a large spoon, so that all the vegetables are covered in oil.
3. Sprinkle the salt, oregano, and basil over the vegetables and mix well again.
4. Place the vegetables and any leftover oil in a large roasting pan. Roast the vegetables for 50 minutes, turning occasionally, or until the vegetables are browned and feel soft when pierced with a fork.
5. Once the vegetables have cooled, put them in the refrigerator in an airtight container.

Vegetable Square

There are some "grown-up" ingredients in this dish, but the taste is not overwhelming. Four different kinds of vegetables make it particularly healthy. I like using it as a "bread": I slice a square in half horizontally and put a little cheese or flavored cream cheese in the middle. Makes 9 to 18 squares.

6 ounce-jar marinated artichokes, reserving marinade
1 medium zucchini, grated (about 2 cups)
1 medium carrot, shredded
1 medium red pepper, finely chopped
1 small onion, minced
2 eggs
⅓ cup feta cheese
¼ cup water
3 tablespoons reserved artichoke marinade
1 cup whole wheat flour
2 teaspoons baking powder
1 teaspoon dried oregano

1. Preheat the oven to 375° F. Grease a 9-inch-square baking pan.
2. Coarsely chop the artichoke hearts. In a mixing bowl combine the artichokes, zucchini, carrot, red pepper, and onion.
3. In a separate bowl combine the eggs, feta, water, and marinade. Add to the vegetables and mix well.
4. Add the flour, baking powder, and oregano to the vegetable mix and blend well.
5. Pour the vegetable batter in the prepared baking pan and smooth over the top a bit. Bake for 30 minutes. Cut into 9 squares; for a young child cut the squares into bars.

Fruits

There are some great ways to pack fruit for lunch, as you will soon see. But if you are going to include a whole fresh fruit, be sure that you wash it, even the fruit you intend to peel. This is great advice, though I have to admit that I have honored this admonition more in the breach than in the observance. But fruits, especially those that are imported from abroad, are sprayed with all sorts of nasty stuff to keep even nastier stuff from entering the country and our food supply. The outside of the fruit can easily contain some leftover residue, and your best bet is to wash it off.

Some fruit, such as bananas and mandarin oranges, come perfectly packaged in their own biodegradable shells. Regular oranges can easily be peeled (though not by a very young child) if you score the orange with a sharp knife (be sure not to cut the flesh). Pack fruits in crush-proof containers: smushed (it's a word at my house) fruit is "yucky looking" (an official kid designation denoting deep disapproval), and you can be sure it will not be eaten.

Dried fruits are great additions to gorp (see Baked Goodies chapter) and granola. And good quality fruit leathers are made of 100 percent fruit, so they are a good sweet snack.

Be especially careful and make sure that your kids can tolerate pineapples, kiwis, mangoes, and papayas. These are the fruits your child is most likely to be allergic to, and it is also possible that their high enzyme content (otherwise an excellent thing) may bother the lining of his or her mouth.

One last word of advice: Don't send an untried fruit to school with your child. It will most likely end up in the trash.

Fruit Universe

Apples

Apples turn brown when peeled or cut and exposed to air. Of all the apple varieties, Cortlands keep from turning dark longer than the other varieties. There are several solutions to this problem:

You could wash the apple, cut it into slices, and dip the apple slices in diluted lemon juice.

Or, wash the apple but do not remove the peel. Quarter it, core it, and reassemble the pieces. Then wrap tightly in plastic wrap. This is not a perfect solution; so if your child is very fussy, it might not be good enough.

A third option is to wash the apple and core it (a melon ball scooper works well) while keeping the apple whole (as if you were going to make baked apples). Stuff the apple with Snack Balls (see Baked Goodies chapter) or with peanut butter. Cap it off with raisins.

You can also buy dried apples, which are chewy and soft.

Apples are high in dietary fiber and contribute vitamin C.

Apricots

A great way to send this delicate fruit, so deliciously loaded with vitamin A, in a lunchbox is to cut it in half, remove the pit, and reassemble it. Wrap tightly in plastic wrap.

Dried apricots are either treated with sulfites to retain their orange color, or are naturally dried and look more brown and leathery.

Apricots are high in vitamins A and C.

Bananas

Bananas are handy because they are so easy to peel, but they need the protection of a hard-sided lunchbox because they mush so easily.

Miniature bananas are more appealing to little kids if the big regular size ones are too big and overwhelming.

If your bananas are getting too ripe to eat, peel them and freeze them in chucks. They are great to have on hand for banana bread and for putting in milk shakes and smoothies.

For a fast, healthy ice cream, take some partly defrosted bananas and some all-fruit spread and process them in a food processor fitted with a steel blade until you have frozen banana mush. Eat this wonderful treat right away.

Dried bananas end up like hard chips (as opposed to most other dried fruits, which are still soft and pliable when dry).

Bananas are a good source of fiber, vitamin C, and potassium.

Berries

All berries are great to add to fruit salads and yogurt, but they will stain clothes, fingers, teeth, and mouth. (Depending on your kids' ages and temperaments, this is either a disaster or "way cool.") They are a good source of vitamin C.

Cherries

Cherries have pits, so you need to make a decision whether to pit them beforehand and have the juice leak out, or leave the task to your child. Cherries will also stain hands and mouth, so that, too, might be a consideration.

Dried cherries are delicious but expensive, and not all of them have the pits removed, so be careful about what you are buying.

Cherries are a good source of vitamin C and fiber.

Cranberries

Fresh cranberries are too tart to eat, but the (sugared) dried varieties are great in a snack. They are a good source of vitamin C.

Dates and Figs

Dried dates and figs are very sweet because they are high in natural sugar, but they make a delicious snack and supply fiber to your diet.

Fresh figs are wonderful but bruise and spoil easily, so eat them soon after you get them home.

Grapefruit

Depending on the variety, grapefruits can be bitter. They hold up very well in fruit salads and are high in vitamin C and provide vitamin A.

Grapes and Raisins

A few clusters of grapes make a convenient snack. If your child dislikes pits, make sure you are buying the seedless grape varieties.

Raisins are a great sweet snack to put in a lunchbox, and a good supply of them in those little boxes is good to have on hand.

Grapes are high in vitamin C. Raisins provide a fair amount of potassium.

Kiwifruit

Kiwis look very pretty in a fruit salad.

For an older child you can cut the kiwi in half, reassemble it, and wrap it tightly in plastic wrap. The soft flesh then can be scooped out with a spoon.

Kiwis are high in vitamin C and are a good source of fiber and potassium.

Mangoes and Papaya

Mangoes are probably my favorite fruit, but they are not the easiest to eat. In a lunchbox, this fruit will work only if you peel it and cut the flesh into little pieces. They are high in vitamin A and a good source of vitamin C.

Papayas can be peeled and seeded and cut into chucks for salad, or cut in half and seeded and wrapped in plastic wrap. The soft papaya flesh can then be scooped out of the skin with a spoon. Papayas are high in vitamin C and provide a good amount of fiber and folate.

Melons

Cantaloupe, muskmelon, and honeydew are juicy and perfect served as slices or in fruit salad. Cantaloupes are high in vitamins C and A and are a good source of potassium and folate. Honeydew melon is high in vitamin C.

Watermelon has lots of seeds (except for the seedless variety). Whether they'll eat it depends on your kids: Some hate removing seeds, others covet them (so that they can spit them out in the school yard and compete in the distance event!). If you do need to remove them, you'll end up with chunks, and a fruit salad is your best option. Watermelon is high in vitamins C and A.

Oranges, Tangerines, and Mandarins

Thick-skinned oranges can be scored deeply and thus peeled easily by an older child.

All except the littlest of fingers can easily peel mandarin oranges. For them, make a little cut (I do this with my fingernail) at the top of the fruit, giving little fingers a grip.

All citrus fruits are perfect in a fruit salad and all citrus is high in vitamin C.

Peaches and Nectarines

If your children don't mind the fuzzy skin of the peach (mine did), you can cut them in half, remove the pit, and reassemble them. Wrap them tightly in plastic wrap. For nectarines this is also an option.

Slices or chunks of peaches and nectarines are great in a fruit salad and provide a good amount of vitamin C.

Pears

This is a very convenient food: All you need to do is remove the core. Just be sure the pear is really ripe; otherwise it has virtually no taste.

After you remove the seeds of the pear, you can stuff the center with a nut butter (almond butter is lovely, if you can find it), reassemble it, and wrap it tightly with plastic wrap.

Pears are a good source of fiber and vitamin C.

Pineapples

You will have to peel and core and chop this pretty fruit before it is ready to eat, but often you can buy it already prepared like that in the supermarket. Either way be sure that you remove all the little pieces of the skin, because their sharp edges will make your mouth sore if you eat them.

If you buy canned pineapple, be sure to get the variety that is packed in light (low-sugar) syrup.

Pineapple is high in vitamin C.

Plums

The pits in plums are often not that easy to remove, so make sure your child is ready to deal with that (small) inconvenience. The one exception to this is the Italian prune plum, which does release its pit easily, so that might be your best option. Plums are high in vitamin C.

Fresh Fruit Kebabs

Kids will eat more when the food looks like fun. For a great presentation, take fruit chunks and skewer them on a toothpick. Another option is to make these kebabs with fruit and alternating pieces of cheese, hard salami, or cubed turkey breast. Fully cooked tortellini also can be skewered. To protect little mouths, use blunt toothpicks or thin coffee stirrer straws. If you are using soft foods and are serving these at home, you can use uncooked spaghetti as skewers. But don't send them to school, because the pasta will go soft.

Variations

- Apple (dipped in diluted lemon juice to keep from discoloring), cheddar cheese, and celery
- Banana, chicken, and jicama
- Carrot, ham, and radishes
- Cherries (remove the pits), salami, and cantaloupe
- Cherry tomatoes and tortellini
- Cucumber, lamb, and red pepper
- Grapefruit sections, orange pieces, and peaches
- Grapes, pineapple cubes, and strawberries
- Honeydew melon and smoked ham (a classic appetizer combination served in the best restaurants)
- Snow peas, water chestnuts, and roast pork
- Turkey breast and mandarin orange
- Watermelon, honeydew melon, and beets
- Zucchini, mild pepper jack cheese, and figs

Fruit Cup

For fruit to make it to lunchtime in an appealing format, you'll need to employ some simple strategies.

In a mixed fruit cup you can keep everything cold by adding some frozen fruit (melon and blueberries are good).

Apples will turn brown when exposed to air, but you can prevent that from happening by dipping them in slightly diluted lemon juice.

Bananas don't do well in a fruit cup; they get mushy. You are better off sending bananas whole. For small children, for whom a big banana is too much, try finding the miniature varieties.

Frozen strawberries also tend to end up mushy when they defrost, so they might not be a good choice.

Blueberries are great but they will turn fingers, teeth, and lips blue, and that might or might not be acceptable to your child.

Canned fruit, in unsweetened syrup, is a good choice, but it will never deliver the vitamins that fresh fruit can, so use the canned varieties only as an occasional treat, or to add to fresh fruit.

You might want to chill the fruit and place it in a chilled thermos: Fruit will stay fresh longer that way.

In the end, only your child will decide what is acceptable and yummy, so experiment at home, before you send something to school.

The following recipe is a rough guide: Just make up your variation. Makes 1 cup.

¼ melon, cut in pieces
¼ cup blueberries
¼ grapefruit, sections cut into thirds
1 plum, cut into pieces
Sprinkle of cinnamon

Mix all the fruits together.

Yogurt and Fruit

You might not think that making your own yogurt lunch is worth it, but I would like you to consider this: For a fraction of the cost of a "ready-made" small yogurt with fruit, you can give your child a homemade one that is lower in sugar and higher in nutrition! Take a good look at the ingredients of the yogurt you are buying and you'll see that you could easily do without those additives.

First of all be sure to buy a plain yogurt that contains "live cultures." Check the label to make sure. These friendly bacteria actually protect the body against some of the infection-causing bacteria.

I use all-fruit spread instead of preserves or jam because it is perfectly sweet without the sugar of a jelly or jam. If you have been eating the commercially sweetened yogurts, you might be used to a very sweet product, so try weaning yourself and your child to a tarter taste little by little.

The frozen fruit in this recipe helps to keep the yogurt cold, but you can add fresh fruit, too. Or pack a frozen juice box or an ice pack with the lunch to keep the yogurt cold, and don't forget a spoon!

Find out from your child if he or she prefers the fruit mixed in or if he or she would like to stir it up from the bottom.

Yogurt itself does not freeze well, but if you like to work ahead, you can freeze serving-size portions of frozen fruit and fruit spread. Makes 1⅓ cups.

1 cup plain, natural, low-fat yogurt
3 tablespoons all-fruit peach spread (no sugar added)
⅓ cup frozen peaches, cut up into bite-size pieces

Mix the ingredients and place into a plastic container with a tight-fitting top.

Variations

- To have a "fruit at the bottom" yogurt lunch, spoon the fruit into the container first, place the all-fruit spread on top of that, and add the yogurt last.

- Instead of peach, try another all-fruit flavor such as strawberry, boysenberry, cherry, or apricot.
- Instead of the frozen peaches, try plums, cherries, or cut up slices of mandarin orange.
- Pack 1/4 cup granola in a separate container to sprinkle over the top of the yogurt. Packing it separately prevents the granola from getting soggy. But check with your child first; some actually like the granola better if it gets mushy.
- If you have see-through containers, make this meal extra pretty by alternately layering the yogurt and fruit.
- If you have a little plain cake leftover, make a "trifle" by layering the cake in the middle.
- Another combination to try is cut up apple, apple butter, and a sprinkle of cinnamon. Put the apple on the bottom to prevent it from browning.

Carrot Apple Salad

Kids always seem to like this colorful salad. You can make it in a few minutes. Makes 2 cups.

1 medium carrot, scraped
1 Granny Smith apple, peeled, cored, and quartered
1 tablespoon fresh-squeezed lemon juice
1 tablespoon maple syrup

In a food processor fitted with the grater blade, grate the carrot and apple. Transfer the mixture to a bowl and sprinkle with the lemon juice and maple syrup. Mix well.

Variation

- Instead of lemon juice and maple syrup, use 2 tablespoons of freshly squeezed orange juice.

Pear and Cottage Cheese

The texture and mild flavor of cottage cheese goes particularly well with pears, but you can substitute any fruit you like. Serves 2 or 3.

¾ cup cottage cheese
½ cup chopped celery
½ cup chopped pears
2 tablespoons raisins
¼ teaspoon cinnamon

Combine the cheese, celery, pears, raisins, and cinnamon in a bowl and mix well.

Variations

- Instead of celery and pears use fruits such as apricots, strawberries, peaches, and seedless grapes cut in half.
- Instead of raisins use other dried fruits.

Poached Pears

A friend who tasted this fruit dish thought it was too fancy for this book. However, it takes only a few minutes to prepare, and you can have the pears poach while you clean the dishes after supper. I like Seckel pears, because they hold their shape well and are a perfect little snack.
Serves 4.

4 Seckel pears, halved and cored
2 cups water
¼ cup honey
1 teaspoon fresh lemon juice
2-inch strip of lemon zest
4 whole cloves
¼ teaspoon ground cinnamon

1. Place all ingredients in a saucepan, and bring to a boil. Turn the heat down and simmer for 15 minutes. Let the pears cool in the poaching liquid.
2. Remove the pears from the poaching liquid only when you are ready to serve them. (Reserve the poaching liquid to add to a smoothie.)
3. To pack them for lunch, put 1 or 2 halves in a plastic container. If you have these at home, you can either serve the pears warm with vanilla ice cream or at room temperature with vanilla yogurt.

COTTAGE CHEESE AND FRUIT IDEAS

If your child likes cottage cheese, fill a small container with a tight-fitting lid with the following combinations:

- Cottage cheese and salad herbs
- Cottage cheese and all-fruit preserves
- Cottage cheese and pineapple ring
- Cottage cheese and peaches, pitted cherries, or other fruits

Sweet Rice Salad

This works well with any kind of leftover rice, but basmati is a particularly tasty and aromatic variety. For some extra protein add the almonds, if your child is old enough. Makes 1½ cups.

1 cup cooked brown basmati rice
¼ cup crushed, drained pineapple
¼ cup raisins
¼ cup chopped almonds (optional)

Dressing

1 tablespoon pineapple juice
1 tablespoon nonfat yogurt
2 teaspoons mayonnaise

1. Place the rice, pineapple, raisins, and almonds, if desired, in a bowl. Mix well.
2. In a shallow dish combine the pineapple juice, yogurt, and mayonnaise. Pour over the rice mixture and stir well. Chill.

Cranberry Relish

What a pity to limit your enjoyment of cranberry relish to Thanksgiving. It is easy to make; cranberries are full of healthy nutrients; and it spices up a turkey, chicken, or roast beef sandwich all year. Makes ¾ cup.

1 cup fresh or frozen cranberries
½ cup brown sugar
1 tablespoon water

1. Put the cranberries, brown sugar, and water in a saucepan and bring to a boil. Turn the heat down to a simmer while the cranberries pop, stirring occasionally.
2. When all the berries have popped, take the saucepan off the heat and let the relish cool. Transfer to a container and refrigerate.

Sweet Peanut Dip

This is an easy sweet dip for fruit. It works equally well as a spread on a piece of toast, too. Peanut butter is relatively high in calories, so don't go overboard. On the other hand, it is a good source of protein, and it encourages you and your children to eat fresh fruits and vegetables. Makes ¼ cup.

2 tablespoons peanut butter
1 tablespoon dry milk powder
1 teaspoon honey
2 tablespoons boiling water

1. In a small bowl combine the peanut butter, milk powder, and honey. Add the boiling water and mix well. Add a little bit more water to get the desired consistency.
2. Use as a dip for pieces of apple, grapes, banana slices, mandarin orange slices, baby carrots, or celery or use as a spread on a toasted bagel or graham crackers. Add a little grated carrot or raisins, too, if you like.

Salads

Common sense, history, and science agree at least on this much: Fruits and vegetables are vital for robust growth, radiant health, abundant energy, and appropriate weight. Many parents complain that their children won't eat vegetables. A scientific study done by the Texas A&M University Department of Horticultural Sciences and the Texas Agricultural Extension Service has proven what many parents have found by experience. If children grow their own vegetables, they are much more likely to eat them. If you have a garden, let your kids develop their green thumbs. There are great books out there about growing vegetables. Some of them are geared directly toward the beginning gardener, so put in some tomato plants, some beans, and a few head of lettuce, and let your child begin to make the connection.

Even in an apartment it might be possible to get some plants growing on a balcony, and a windowsill is a perfect spot for herbs. You can always sprout beans and add the sprouts to a sandwich. I know many people whose New York City apartments are a jungle of avocado plants sprouted from pits left over from their avocado sandwiches.

With so much new information coming out these days, you could well be very confused about which vegetables and fruits you ought to eat. It is really not necessary to know what contains lycopene and how to tell your anthocyanins from your zeaxanthin! What you do need to do is make sure that you feed yourself and your child a good variety of fruits and vegetables.

Dr. David Heber, in a brilliant book entitled *What Color Is Your Diet?*, has divided fruits and vegetables into seven color categories, with each color providing a specific and distinctive set of nutrients. The colors indicate the sorts of nutrients the fruits and vegetables will provide. Include one fruit or vegetable from each group every day in your diet, and you'll be sure to get a good variety of nutrients.

Red Group—tomatoes, pink grapefruit, and watermelon

Red/Purple Group—purple grapes, prunes, cranberries, red beets, red bell pepper, red apples, strawberries, and blueberries

Orange Group—pumpkins, carrots, sweet potatoes, mangoes, apricots, and cantaloupes

Orange/Yellow Group—oranges, tangerines, peaches, lemons, pineapple, papayas, and nectarines

Yellow/Green—green peas, green beans, spinach, green peppers, cucumbers, kiwi, honeydew, zucchini, corn, and avocados

White/Green Group—garlic, onions, celery, leeks, and mushrooms

Green Group—broccoli, cabbage, and bok choy

Vegetable Universe

Here is a list of some vegetables that would be good to include in a lunchbox.

Artichokes

This might not be the first vegetable you think of when you are looking to pack a lunch for your child, but maybe you should think again. If you eat artichokes at home, there is no reason they cannot be brought to school.

Be sure to clip all the sharp pointy ends off the artichokes and then boil the artichoke leaves until they are soft, about 40 minutes. Obviously, you will have to teach your children at home how to eat the artichoke. Show them how to pull off the leaves, dip the meaty ends of the leaves in a sauce, and suck and scrape off the soft bottom half of the leaf with their teeth. Then comes the more difficult part of taking off the last few light yellow leaves and scooping out the fuzzy and prickly choke portion with a spoon. Once that is gone, the delicious artichoke bottom is left. Depending on the personality of your child, this exotic vegetable could be a great hit. Though the traditional dipping sauce is melted butter, any kind of dipping sauce or salad dressing could be used.

Artichokes supply vitamins A and C as well as potassium.

Asparagus

If your child eats this vegetable at home, why not serve it for a school lunch? Although this is traditionally a spring vegetable, it now pops up all through the year. Snapping the tough bottoms off a fresh asparagus is a good chore for even a relatively young child. After you have steamed asparagus for dinner, you can place some of them in a plastic bag for lunch the next day. Pack a small container of salad dressing with it. For an older child, you can pour Italian dressing over cut-up and steamed asparagus for a tasty and healthy salad.

Asparagus is a good source of vitamins A and C and has a little calcium and iron, too.

Avocado

Avocado is a mild vegetable that when mashed up to a smooth paste and flavored with a little salt and pepper is a perfect and nutritious spread. Always include a little lemon juice in an avocado dish, so that it will keep its bright green color. Try making a flour tortilla wrap with mashed avocado, chopped cucumbers and tomatoes, and refried beans.

Avocado has the highest vegetable source of vitamin E.

Beans

Green beans are perfect dipping vegetables. Lightly steamed they are crunchy and a pretty green color and they will keep for a few days. Because they are great in so many dishes, you can steam a lot of them at the beginning of the week and then add them to dishes all during the week as well as to the lunchbox. They are great to stuff in wraps because of their shape.

Beans are available throughout the year and their cousin, the yellow wax bean, is available mainly in the summer.

Green beans supply vitamin A and potassium.

Shell beans such as fava beans and lima beans are great additions to any mixed salads. Try mixing them with chopped tomatoes and crumbled feta cheese and sprinkle some oregano over all. Shelling beans is a fun job for children, so let them help you.

Dried beans come in many varieties, and having all these pretty colors in glass jars will liven up the decor in your kitchen. Dried beans can find their way into so many dishes: garbanzo beans in hummus, split peas in soup, pinto beans in a Mexican dip. You might find the beans more digestible if you throw away the soaking water for the dried beans before you cook them in fresh water.

If you want to make a pretty and easy kitchen gift, you can layer different beans in a glass container. Add a recipe for bean soup or a pretty ribbon, and you have a great homemade gift your child can be proud to give any adult friend.

To help your children with their sorting skills, you can mix up two or more different kinds of beans, and let them sort the beans out while they keep you company in the kitchen. You can make it easy by mixing different sizes of beans, such as garbanzo and lentils, or you can make it hard by mixing same-size beans, such as green and yellow split peas.

It is fun and educational to sprout beans: Magically a bean transforms itself into a little edible plant right before your eyes. There are excellent books on sprouting by Steve "the sprout man" Meyerowitz that I highly recommend (see Resources). Tuck sprouts into salads, sandwiches, and pita pockets.

Shell beans and dried beans are a great vegetarian source of protein as well as iron and potassium.

Beets

Beets are packed with healthful components and have a sweet and mild taste. The only reason I hesitate recommending them more highly is because the beautiful red stains are just about permanent. But by all means, eat them at home.

Because of its superb ability to stain, beet juice is a great, nonchemical way to stain white food red. Try a few drops in frosting, mayonnaise, yogurt, or baked goods.

Beets are a good source of folate, a B vitamin.

Broccoli and Cauliflower

Maybe you remember a certain U.S. president insisting that now that he was in high office he didn't have to eat his broccoli if he didn't feel like it! I blame his mommy for this irresponsible attitude, and I hope you will do better with your brood.

Raw or lightly steamed broccoli and cauliflower are easy vegetables to like. They are great for dipping or can find their way into a chopped salad. And they help to protect against some types of cancer.

Cream of broccoli soup can warm a cold belly on a bitter winter's day. If your child likes cooked cauliflower, you can use the same recipes for cream of broccoli soup and substitute cauliflower instead.

A few little white or green "trees" provide your child with vitamins A and C.

Cabbage

Though cooked cabbage is not a popular food, we all eat it gladly in coleslaw. In its simplest form, you can make coleslaw by shredding some cabbage and carrots and moistening the mixture with a little mayonnaise and yogurt.

Shredded cabbage is also a great addition in tomato-based soups; the tomato somehow mellows out the assertive taste of the cabbage.

It is worth making an effort to add cabbage to various salads, soups, and sandwiches because this vegetable has such powerful health-giving properties. It is also a good source of vitamin C and fiber.

Carrots

This is probably close to the top of everybody's list of favorite vegetables.

This versatile vegetable can either be the star of or play a great supporting role in a wide variety of dishes. Baby carrots are easy to dip in dressing; grated carrot is usually well accepted in sandwiches and salads and it easily can blend into soups. It is also one of the few vegetables that can find its way into desserts.

Carrots supply great amounts of beta-carotene and vitamin A and are the traditional protectors of our eyesight.

Celery

Together with carrots, celery is a favorite vegetable for dipping. Because of its shape it is also the star of the Ants on a Log recipe found later in this chapter. And because of its reliable, wilt-proof crunch, it is also a great addition to chicken and turkey salad. If you feel like having a crunchy salad, try a combination of chopped celery and Granny Smith apples.

Celery gives you vitamin C and potassium.

Corn

There are so many wonderful ways to eat this vegetable. Corn flour can be used for corn muffins, popcorn is a perennial favorite, and corn itself is an excellent addition to chopped salads and soups.

Although it is easy to grab for the frozen and canned corn, it is actually very easy to scrape off the kernels from leftover steamed corn. And it's much tastier and healthier, too.

Corn is a cheerful addition to a bean salad, but you can come up with many more variations. Try a salad of finely chopped green pepper, corn kernels, and shredded cheddar cheese.

Corn is a good source of vitamin C.

Cucumbers

Cukes are loved for their cool crunch and mild flavor. In the Middle East, eating a salad of diced cucumbers, tomatoes, and onions seasoned with a little olive oil, a squeeze of lemon juice, and some salt and pepper is a very healthy daily habit. You can add a little chopped smoked turkey to include some protein in this salad. Or cut cucumbers into spears, discarding the seeds in the middle, so they can be used as finger foods.

Cucumbers are a good source of vitamin C.

Greens

I hate to be the one to say something bad about a vegetable, but there is really next to nothing good that can be said about iceberg lettuce, however popular it is. The healthful benefits of lettuce are in the dark green–colored part, and the anemic color of iceberg should tell you that it is the white sugar of vegetables. Experiment with the many dark green lettuces that you can find, like romaine, spinach, Boston, and the mixed baby lettuces that are now common in supermarkets.

For a lot of kids, big lettuce leaves are unappealing in a salad, so chop them up into small pieces so they can be eaten in one mouthful.

Green leaves can serve a great role in the making of sandwiches in that they provide a waterproof barrier between bread and a filling such as tuna fish, which could otherwise turn the bread soggy. Wash lettuce leaves at one go, and store the dried leaves loosely in a plastic bag for a few days. That way you will always have them ready for lunches and dinners.

Greens are good sources of vitamin A and fiber.

Peas and Snow Peas

Shelling peas is the perfect job for a kid: Pulling the string and finding all those peas snugly nestled in the pod is something that still brings a smile to my face. Once your child gets the hang of it, you can even send unshelled peas to school. Fresh peas can be mixed with carrots cut into little cubes for a fresh version of the standard peas and carrots side dish.

Snow peas can be eaten just as they are, and they are about the easiest vegetable to tuck into a lunchbox with a little dip on the side.

Peas are chock-full of vitamins A and C and various B vitamins.

Peppers

I am not sure any other vegetable comes in so many different colors, but you can find bell peppers in red, green, yellow, black, and orange. If chopped, they make a colorful addition to any salad. Or you can cut them into strips for dipping.

Red peppers have a milder and sweeter taste than green ones. Chopped red peppers, fresh green peas, and goat cheese make a great salad.

Bell peppers are a good source of vitamins C and B_6.

Potatoes and Sweet Potatoes

Potatoes are usually classified as a starch, but they are, of course, a root vegetable. Potatoes cannot be eaten raw, but they are a great leftover once they are cooked. Because of potatoes' bland taste, potato salad is a great side dish to add some extra vegetables to. Bell peppers, radishes, celery, peas, carrots, and corn can all be mixed in to make the potato salad more nutritious. Potatoes are high in vitamin C and potassium.

Sweet potatoes supply excellent quantities of vitamin A, and they can be substituted for regular potatoes in many recipes. Cooked and cubed sweet potatoes can be tossed with orange sections and dressed with balsamic vinegar dressing for an unusual salad.

Radishes

Radishes have a little bit of a bite to them, and if your child likes them, they are a great addition to the lunchbox: red, round, cute, and squish-proof. A chopped salad of radishes, hard-boiled eggs, and a few scallions moistened with a little Russian dressing is a nice change of pace.

Radishes are a good source of vitamin C.

Tomatoes

Tomatoes are one of the most popular of vegetables. They are great sliced on sandwiches or chopped in salads, and cherry tomatoes you can just pop into your mouth! Little cherry tomatoes are also great on skewers, or you can cut off the cap, scoop out the inside with a melon scooper, and stuff it with a little flavored cream cheese, tuna salad, or chicken salad. Place the cap back on and you have a little cherry tomato surprise.

Tomatoes supply vitamins A, C, and E.

Zucchini

This is a nice mild-mannered vegetable that you can mix into lots of different salads. It lends a mild crunch to any chopped salad, and it's high in vitamin C.

CROUTONS

Croutons are a fun addition to a salad. All you need is some dried-out bread—for instance, crusts or slices of French bread—and olive oil or garlic-flavored olive oil.

With a food brush, brush a little of the oil on the bread crusts or slices. Place them on a baking sheet and toast them in the oven or toaster oven. When the bread is nicely browned, carefully turn over and brush on a little more oil. Toast briefly again. Cool and store in an airtight container.

Chef's Salad

Open to endless variation, this is a great way to use up small quantities of lettuce, meat, cheese, and egg. There is no set recipe for this. Serves 1 or more.

Lettuce
Tomato
Cucumber
Cheese
Cold cuts
Hard-boiled egg
Dressing

Place the lettuce in a plastic bowl. Layer on the rest of the salad ingredients. Top off with the cheese, meat, and, finally, sliced hard-boiled egg. Pack the dressing separately.

Chicken Salad

Chicken salad is a surefire winner: celery adds crunch and grapes add sweetness. Because you control the amount of mayonnaise you put in, this is a much healthier version than what you buy at the supermarket. If you like, line the bread with lettuce leaves so that the salad does not make the bread soggy. Makes 2 cups.

1 chicken breast, cooked
½ cup chopped celery
½ cup chopped grapes
1 teaspoon mayonnaise
1 teaspoon mustard vinaigrette

In a large bowl blend all the ingredients. Chill.

Tuna Salad Niçoise

This tuna fish salad is a more grown-up version of the tuna salad in the sandwich chapter. When your growing child is ready for olives and a little more flavor, try this variation. I suggest that you pack it separately, in a plastic container, with a roll on the side. Makes 2 cups.

6 ounces water-packed tuna fish, drained well
1 cup finely chopped celery (about 2 stalks)
½ cup finely chopped red pepper
2 tablespoons chopped black olives
1 tablespoon minced sweet onion
1 tablespoon mayonnaise
1 tablespoon yogurt
1 teaspoon apple cider vinegar
¼ teaspoon salt, or to taste
Freshly ground pepper, to taste
2 cups torn lettuce leaves

1. Put the tuna fish in a mixing bowl and add the celery, red pepper, olives, and onion. Mix well. Add the mayonnaise, yogurt, vinegar, salt, and pepper. Mix well.
2. Line a plastic container with lettuce leaves and put the salad on top. Pack cold.

Waldorf Salad

The traditional Waldorf Salad uses walnuts as an essential component of the taste, so I have included them here. However, if you are serving this to a younger child, consider omitting the nuts (because of the potential choking hazard).

Crushed pineapple freezes well. If you think you might like to make Waldorf Salad frequently, freeze two-tablespoon portions of pineapple in ice cube containers. Remove the pineapple chunks when they are fully frozen and place them in a marked plastic bag for future use.

If you are using a tart apple, you will need a little less of the lemon juice. But don't omit it completely since it will prevent discoloration of the apple. Makes 1½ cups.

1 crisp apple
½ to 1 teaspoon fresh lemon juice
1 stalk celery, chopped
¼ cup chopped walnuts
2 tablespoons crushed pineapple
1 tablespoon 1 percent fat yogurt
1 teaspoon mayonnaise

1. Chop the apple into small chunks, place in a mixing bowl, and sprinkle with the lemon juice. Add the celery, walnuts, and pineapple. Mix well.
2. In a separate bowl, mix the yogurt and mayonnaise. Pour over the apple mixture and blend well.

Spinach Dip

This is a delicious way to get your children to eat spinach. You can serve it as a dip, or it also works well as a spread (try it on a tomato sandwich!). You can easily double this recipe. Serves 4 to 5.

5 ounces frozen chopped spinach (half a package)
1 cup light sour cream
1 scallion, white part and 2 inches of the green part cut into 1-inch pieces
1½ teaspoons Worcestershire sauce

1. Cook the spinach according to package directions. Place the spinach into a colander and squeeze out the moisture.
2. In a food processor fitted with the steel blade, place the spinach, sour cream, scallion, and Worcestershire sauce. Process until the spinach is chopped into small pieces. Scrape down the sides of the bowl and process again to blend well.
3. Place in a covered container in the refrigerator. Serve with little carrots and whole wheat crackers or spread it on a sandwich.

Celery with Blue Cheese Dressing

This is probably not suitable for very young children, but once they are old enough for the strong taste of blue cheese, it makes a great vegetable and dip combo. Blue cheese is not a low-fat food, but this homemade dip is better than the commercial versions, and if your child ends up eating some more vegetables because of it, well, then it might be worth it. Serves 1.

4 celery sticks, cut lengthwise into thin stalks
Blue cheese dressing

For the dressing

¼ cup blue cheese
¼ cup nonfat yogurt

1. Place the cheese in a bowl and mash with a fork. Add the yogurt and mix very well. Chill.
2. Wrap the celery in plastic wrap. Package the dressing separately in a container with a secure top.

Cucumber Salad

The dressing will make the cucumbers wilt and give them a nice and soft texture. Try this salad at home first to see if your child likes it. Serves 2.

1 cucumber, peeled and sliced thin
2 teaspoons apple cider vinegar
⅓ cup water
1 tablespoon snipped fresh dill
½ teaspoon white sugar
Salt and pepper to taste

1. Combine all the ingredients and let them marinate for at least 1 hour in the refrigerator.
2. Drain off the dressing and serve cold.

Ants on a Log

Here's a great way to sneak a vegetable into your children's lunch or snack, especially at Halloween! If your kids are old enough (to understand that plastic is not for eating), consider buying a package of decorative black plastic ants, and for Halloween you can then put on some "real" ants.

This is a fun lunch to make with your child, since the best way to get the nut butter in the celery is with your fingers.

This recipe makes one "log."

1 celery stick
1 to 2 tablespoons peanut butter
1 to 2 tablespoons raisins

Using your fingers, fill the hollow part of the celery with peanut butter. Line the raisin "ants" up on the sticky peanut butter, pressing them in a bit. Wrap tightly in plastic wrap.

Variation

- Instead of the raisins, dip the peanut butter side in shredded, unsweetened coconut. What could you call this, Snow on a Log?

Bean Dip

Your children might like Mexican foods, but not the hot taste, so buy your salsa to match their needs. This high-protein dip can also be used as a spread on sandwiches. Makes 1 cup.

1 cup cooked canned pinto beans, drained
3 ounces salsa
¼ cup low-fat sour cream

1. In a food processor fitted with the steel blade, blend all the ingredients until smooth.
2. Serve as a dip with vegetables, as a spread in a wrap, or with some low-fat baked corn chips.

Mexican Layered Beans

This is a variation on a popular party dip. If you use lots of veggies, this is actually a very healthy dish that you can let your child eat often. I hesitate to give you proportions because you can make this entirely to your family's taste. Low-fat corn chips (see the next page) are great to scoop this up with. Makes 1 serving.

Canned pinto beans, drained, mashed, and seasoned with salt to taste
Red onion, minced
Chopped tomato
Chopped green pepper
Canned corn, drained
Salsa
Shredded cheddar cheese
Reduced-fat sour cream

In a plastic container layer the ingredients in the order listed.

Variation

- Season the mashed pinto beans with some cumin.

Salsa with Low-Fat Chips

When you make fresh salsa you are including all sorts of vegetables. Together with low-fat tortilla chips, this makes a fine addition to a lunch. If your child likes the heat, you can always add more chiles. Taking the peel off the tomatoes is a small extra step (to be done by an adult) and makes the texture of the salsa smoother. Makes 2 cups.

4 tomatoes
¼ cup chopped onion
1 clove garlic
1 tablespoon olive oil
1 tablespoon dried basil leaves
1 green chile, stem and seeds removed
Salt and black pepper

1. In a large pot bring 2 quarts of water to a boil. Carefully place the tomatoes in the water and let them cook for a few minutes, until you can see the skin "pop." Take the tomatoes out of the water and let them cool. Slip the peels off.
2. In a food processor fitted with the steel blade, process the onion, garlic, oil, and basil leaves until smooth. Scrape down the sides. Add the green chile, and process until finely mixed.
3. Quarter the tomatoes and add them to the food processor. Process until the mixture is well blended but still coarse.

Low-Fat Chips

The chips you buy in the supermarket are loaded with salt and unhealthy oil. But you can make these low-fat chips quickly and be sure that you are giving your child a much better snack. If you serve them with Bean Dip, the Mexican Layered Beans dish, or Hummus (see recipes in this book), you will be complementing the protein in the corn with the protein in the beans to make a nutritious combination.

An oil mister for these chips and other recipes comes in handy. This wonderful device allows you to take any healthy oil you have on hand and spray foods with a light, even coating of oil.

Corn tortillas
Olive oil

1. Cut corn tortillas into sixths and place them in a single layer on a lightly greased (sprayed) cookie sheet. Spray the tortillas lightly with cooking spray or olive oil. Sprinkle lightly with a little salt.
2. Bake at 350° F for 10 minutes, or until lightly browned.

Green Beans Vinaigrette

Green beans, also known as string beans or French beans, are an ideal vegetable, if you ask me. There's not much waste and they have the perfect shape for dipping. The same can be said of wax beans. It is certainly easy enough to take a few leftover green beans and marinate them, overnight, in a mild vinaigrette. I use rice vinegar because of its mild taste.

In the morning, lift them out of the vinaigrette and place them in a plastic container for some green finger food. Serves 2 grown-ups or 4 kids.

½ pound green beans
½ cup olive oil
1 tablespoon rice vinegar
1 tablespoon coarse Dijon-style mustard
¼ teaspoon salt

1. Put a steamer basket at the bottom of a saucepan and add water up to but not beyond the bottom of the steamer. Bring the water to a boil.
2. Wash the green beans and cut the tips off the ends. Place the beans in the steamer and cover. Let them steam for about 4 minutes, or until they turn bright green.
3. Meanwhile, put the oil, vinegar, mustard, and salt in a blender and blend until emulsified.
4. When the green beans are done steaming, drain them in a colander. Place the hot beans in a dish and pour the vinaigrette over them, turning the beans to cover them. Let the dish cool to room temperature and cover the beans with plastic wrap. Let them marinate overnight in the refrigerator.
5. To serve, drain the beans and eat cold or at room temperature.

Variations

- You can zip up the vinaigrette by adding a small clove of pressed garlic and blending well.
- A bit of fresh pepper or minced Vidalia onion is also great if your child likes it.

Vegetable Cheese Pasta Salad

It is easy to see that this is a great lunch dish to make right after you have eaten a pasta dinner. There are as many variations on this salad as there are leftovers. You can use any cheese your child likes, except American cheese; just about any combination of vegetables will do; and you can use other dressings if you like.

The real trick to a pretty vegetable pasta salad is to use small pasta shapes and to chop the rest of the ingredients small, too, so you can get a little of all the different tastes in every forkful. Makes 2 cups.

½ cup dry or 1 cup cooked ditalini or other small pasta shapes
⅓ cup diced red pepper
⅓ cup diced and steamed green beans
⅓ cup diced feta cheese
⅓ cup low-fat yogurt
1 tablespoon dry buttermilk powder
⅛ teaspoon salt

1. Cook the pasta according to the instructions on the package.
2. In a bowl combine the cooked pasta, red pepper, green beans, and feta cheese. Mix well.
3. In a small bowl mix the yogurt, buttermilk powder, and salt. Pour the dressing over the pasta mixture and blend well. Chill.

Variations

- Use cheddar, Monterey Jack, or any other favorite cheese (except American). You can also try mozzarella, but the result might be too bland.
- Cooked or steamed vegetable choices include asparagus, broccoli, artichoke hearts, and wax beans.
- Raw vegetable choices include tomatoes, whole cherry tomatoes, and green peppers.
- You might like to try a balsamic vinaigrette or Russian dressing.
- Add a tablespoonful of minced Vidalia onion, parsley, dill, or basil to enhance the flavor.

Potato Salad

A picnic classic, the potato salad is a great dish. The supermarket/deli variation is not really the healthiest kind, so make this from scratch and keep control over your nutrition and calorie intake. Serves 2 to 4.

14 small new potatoes, boiled
½ cup olive oil
¼ cup apple cider vinegar
¼ cup Dijon mustard
1 small clove garlic
1 teaspoon dried oregano

1. Put the potatoes in a bowl. Set aside.
2. Put the oil, vinegar, mustard, garlic, and oregano in a blender container and blend for 30 seconds. Pour ¼ cup of the vinaigrette over the potatoes and let them marinate overnight.

Variations

Try adding some of the following if you like:

- 1 hard-boiled egg, chopped
- ¼ cup shredded cheese
- ½ cup vegetables such as chopped red or green pepper, steamed and chopped broccoli, chopped tomato, or chopped celery
- ¼ cup chopped meat such as roast beef, salami, ham, turkey, or chicken

Vegetable Rice Salad

Rice is a great neutral foil for exciting salads. If you start off with brown rice, you get a nice bit of fiber and some vitamin Bs as well. Adapt the recipes to include the ingredients you know your child likes and eats.

The easy way to make this salad is right after you have dinner. Take the leftover rice, chop any leftover salad vegetables (including the spinach or other greens), moisten the salad with some dressing, mix it up, place the salad in an airtight container in the fridge, and voilà—lunch for tomorrow is waiting. Serves 2.

- 1 cup cooked brown rice
- 1 hard-boiled egg, chopped, or ½ cup chopped cooked chicken
- 1 cup chopped celery
- ½ cup chopped cucumber
- ½ cup low-fat yogurt
- ¼ cup mayonnaise
- 1 teaspoon honey mustard

Mix all the ingredients in a bowl and chill.

Variation

- Instead of the yogurt dressing, moisten the salad with a mild vinaigrette.

Soups

Nothing warms you to the bone like a bowl of soup or stew. Not only is it comforting, but broths actually contain health-giving properties. I don't think of making soups as a separate cooking chore. It is a way of processing left-overs and scraps to make the next nourishing meal. You can have soup simmering on the stove while you do your evening chores, and suddenly you have a meal that is healthier and faster than you could possibly buy at a fast-food place.

I have included a from-scratch chicken soup recipe in this chapter, but let me explain my "leftover soup methodology" first. I keep a plastic bag in the freezer and put into it all clean potato peelings (except the peels that are green), tough dark green leaves from leeks and scallions, carrot scrapings (of course, I wash the carrots thoroughly), large outer celery stalks, parsley stems, mushroom stems, all sorts of other vegetables left over from dinners, and the giblets from the chickens I buy whole (except for the livers, which I freeze separately).

After I have served a roasted chicken, for instance, I pick all the remaining meat off the carcass for chicken salad. Then I put the carcass and the vegetables I have saved in the plastic bag into a big stockpot with lots of water. I add a few bay leaves and some salt and pepper, and I put it on the stove over a low flame. After the soup comes to a boil, I let it simmer for 5 minutes and then skim the fat from the surface. Then I let the stock simmer for a few hours more (if it is in the evening, I set a timer so that I'll remember to check the soup).

After a few hours I take the soup off the heat, let it cool down a bit, and strain the broth. If there was a lot of meat on the chicken carcass, you might want to pick it off, but after all that time simmering, there will not be much flavor left. (Then again, your child might not actually care too much about that and prefer meat that is nice and soft.) Throw away the vegetables and giblets (unless your grandmother gave you a good recipe for the giblets). Place the broth in a container in the refrigerator. Once it is cold, the chicken fat will have congealed on the top, and you can skim it off quite easily. What you have now is a flavorful, healthy broth that will make every soup or stew you add it to more delicious.

Though this is not politically correct, you might want to reserve some of the chicken fat to fry up some chopped onion with the defrosted chicken livers you have saved. When the chicken livers are done, you can puree them in a food processor fitted with a steel blade. This pâté, or chopped liver, is delicious on crackers and toast.

Though it is entirely possible, not to mention delicious, to make straight vegetable broth, the gelatinous aspect of soup comes from simmering bones for a long time; a pure vegetable broth will be very thin in comparison.

Be careful when you reheat soup to pour into your child's thermos. If you ladle very hot soup into a thermos in the morning, it will most probably still be really hot at lunch, and you don't want your child to get burnt.

Soup is a great addition to your diet. Teach your child the pleasure of blowing cold air over each spoonful to cool it down. Eat your soup slowly and enjoy your low-calorie lunch.

Alphabet Soup

A kid staple, alphabet soup is very easy to prepare, and you can make sure it contains only the healthful ingredients you want to feed your kids. You can also substitute and omit vegetables so that only your kids' favorites end up in the soup.

This makes a large pot of soup, but it freezes well, so it makes sense to prepare a large batch. Serves 12.

8 cups vegetable broth, homemade chicken broth, beef stock, or canned chicken broth
3 cups tomato juice or vegetable juice
2 onions, quartered
1 clove garlic
3 carrots, peeled and cut to ¼-inch dice
1 large potato, peeled and cut to ¼-inch dice
1 cup alphabet noodles
Salt and pepper to taste
Chopped parsley (optional)

1. In a large stockpot bring the broth to a boil.
2. Meanwhile put 2 cups of the tomato or vegetable juice, the onions, and garlic in a blender and puree. Add the puree to the broth with the remaining juice. Bring the liquid back to a boil.
3. Add the carrots, potato, and noodles and cook until the vegetables are soft, about 10 minutes. Season with salt and pepper to taste.
4. Serve hot with parsley sprinkled on top or cool and then freeze for later use.

Variations

- You can vary the noodle shapes. If you want, cook the noodles separately and add them at the end of the cooking time to heat through.
- You can also add other vegetables, such as turnips (at the same time as the carrots) or peas (if canned, add them at the very end of the cooking time just to heat through. If frozen, cook them separately and add them at the end of the cooking period).

Chicken Soup

I rarely make chicken soup from scratch. In my house it is generally the natural follow-up meal to a roasted chicken, as I told you in the introduction to this chapter. But here is the "from scratch" recipe, and it couldn't be easier! This is the sort of recipe where the proportions of things just don't much matter. Throw in loads of celery if you like it; add a couple of minced garlic cloves, why don't you; and, by all means, leave out the carrots if you don't happen to like them.

If you start this soup right after dinner, you will have a giant pot ready by the time you have cleaned up the dishes and finished watching the evening news. Serves 8.

4 pounds chicken, cut up into pieces, except for the livers
8 cups water
1 teaspoon salt
2 onions, chopped
2 celery stalks, chopped
2 medium carrots, chopped
2 garlic cloves, minced (optional)
⅓ cup minced fresh parsley

1. Put the chicken, water, and salt in a large pot and bring to a boil. Turn down the heat and simmer, covered, for 30 minutes.
2. Add the vegetables and bring the soup back to a simmer. Cook for 20 more minutes.
3. Cool the soup until you can handle the chicken comfortably. Remove the chicken and discard the skin. Pull the meat from the bones and cut it into small pieces. Stir the meat back into the soup.
4. If you want to eat the soup right away, skim off as much surface fat as you comfortably can and reheat the soup to boiling. Serve with parsley sprinkled on top.
5. If you are reserving the soup, let the soup cool and then refrigerate it. Before reheating the soup, skim off the congealed fat on the surface. Reheat the soup to boiling and serve with parsley sprinkled on top.

Cream of Tomato Soup

This is a classic and still a favorite soup, which you can make from scratch in a matter of minutes. A steaming thermos filled with soup is sure to satisfy a hungry child.

The magic of making a perfectly smooth white-sauce base with no additional fat is in the technique: The nonstick pan must already be hot, the flour and milk mixture must be completely mixed, and you must continuously stir the sauce as it is getting thick.

If your child dislikes little pieces of onion in the soup, strain the mixture as you pour it from the blender into the hot pan. Serves 1.

1 cup milk
1 tablespoon whole wheat flour
½ teaspoon instant vegetable broth
½ teaspoon olive oil
½ cup minced onion
½ cup tomato sauce
Salt and pepper to taste

1. Put the milk, flour, and vegetable broth in a blender and blend until smooth.
2. In a large nonstick frying pan, heat the oil and sauté the onion until transparent and just beginning to brown.
3. Transfer the onion to the milk mixture and blend for 30 seconds while keeping the pan hot on a medium flame. Pour the onion-milk mixture at once into the pan and turn the heat up high. Stir continuously until the mixture comes to a boil.
4. Add the tomato sauce and turn the heat down. Simmer for 5 minutes.
5. Add salt and pepper to taste.

Vegetable Soup

This is a recipe open to endless variation, and I can't imagine that any two batches of vegetable soup are ever remotely the same. You can alternate beef, chicken, or vegetable broth, or make the soup with water and add miso or tamari to impart a salty broth flavor. Virtually all vegetables and grains can be tossed into the soup, so it is a great way to use up leftovers. The real magic of this soup lies in having all vegetables chopped into small quarter-inch pieces, so that you get a mix of several vegetables in every bite. Though the recipe reads as if I have every ingredient chopped and ready for the adding, the reality of soup making is that as the broth simmers away, I keep chopping and adding, starting with the root vegetables and ending with the herbs. This is a great dish to make when you're having a long heart-to-heart with someone in the kitchen!

This version is a little fiery because of the hot peppers; feel free to omit them if you have young children who don't like the heat. I added quinoa to this recipe because it is an easy-to-digest high-protein grain. Rinse the quinoa well before you add it to the soup, to get rid of the bitter coating. When this grain is cooked through, it becomes transparent and has a white ring. Serves 8.

8 cups water, vegetable broth, or chicken stock
1 cup quinoa, rinsed well
½ teaspoon olive oil
1 onion, chopped
2 cloves garlic, minced
1 large potato, scrubbed clean and chopped
1 large carrot, scrubbed clean and chopped
1 cup chopped green beans
2 celery stalks, chopped
1 red pepper, seeded and chopped
½ green pepper, seeded and chopped
2 jalapeño peppers, seeded and minced
2 scallions, both green and white, chopped
½ cup minced fresh parsley

1 tablespoon dried oregano
1½ teaspoons dried basil leaves
Salt and pepper to taste
Miso or tamari (optional)

1. Put the water or broth in a large stockpot over moderate heat. Add the quinoa and stir.
2. Meanwhile, in a small pan heat the oil and sauté the onion until the onion is transparent. Add the garlic and sauté until the garlic is fragrant, about 1 minute. Add the garlic and onion mixture to the stockpot.
3. Add the potato, carrot, green beans, celery, red pepper, green pepper, jalapeño pepper, scallions, parsley, oregano, and basil, one at a time, as you wash, clean, and chop each vegetable.
4. Keep the soup at a low simmer until all the vegetables and quinoa are cooked through. The time will vary and will depend on how small you cut the root vegetables. Add salt, pepper, miso, or tamari to taste.

Cream of Corn Soup

I use white flour in this recipe because the whole wheat flour leaves little dark flecks in the sauce. This recipe makes one serving, but feel free to double, triple, or quadruple it. Just go light on the instant vegetable broth and add only half of it while making the soup; add the rest of it to taste at the end. Serves 1.

½ teaspoon olive oil
¼ cup minced onion
¼ cup minced celery
1 cup milk
1 tablespoon unbleached all-purpose flour
1 teaspoon instant vegetable broth
½ cup canned corn, drained

1. In a large nonstick frying pan, heat the oil and sauté the onion and celery until the onion is transparent and just beginning to brown.
2. Meanwhile, put the milk, flour, and vegetable broth powder in a blender and blend until smooth. Add the corn and blend for a few seconds until the corn is reduced to small pieces.
3. Add the corn mixture to the hot pan all at once, turn the heat up to high, and continue stirring the soup until it comes to a boil.
4. Turn the heat down and, stirring occasionally, let the soup simmer for 5 minutes.

Zucchini Soup

This is as simple as it gets, with no complicated tastes to overwhelm a young child or a person recuperating from a cold. This is also a perfect vegetarian answer to chicken soup when someone is feeling weak and has no appetite. Serves 1.

1 cup water or chicken broth

½ small zucchini, cut in ½-inch slices

1. In a small saucepan, steam the zucchini over 1/2 cup of water or broth until the zucchini is soft, about 5 minutes. Let cool a little.
2. Place the rest of the water or broth in a blender and add the steamed zucchini and the leftover steaming water or broth. Blend until completely smooth.
3. Heat the soup until hot and serve.

Split Pea Vegetable Soup

This hearty soup is great in the wintertime. I make it as a vegetarian meal, but some chopped leftover ham would be a wonderful addition. Serves 4.

4 cups water

1 cup split peas, rinsed and picked over

1 potato, peeled and cut into ½-inch pieces

1 large carrot, peeled and cut into ½-inch pieces

1 onion, chopped

1 clove garlic, minced

1 bay leaf

1. In a large pot combine the water, peas, potato, carrot, onion, garlic, and bay leaf. Bring to a boil; turn down the heat and cover. Simmer gently for 2 hours, stirring occasionally. You will need to lower the heat and stir more often toward the end of the cooking time, or else the bottom will scorch. Add more water if you like your soup thinner. You will know that the soup is done when the peas have "melted."
2. Remove the bay leaf before serving.

Minestrone

If you have any leftover minestrone from your family dinner, plan to send it to school in a wide-mouthed thermos. Minestrone freezes well, so make the full amount. Serves 8.

1 egg
¼ cup milk
½ cup flavored breadcrumbs
1 pound ground beef
1 tablespoon minced fresh parsley
6 cups beef broth
1 28-ounce can crushed tomatoes
2 cups shredded cabbage
1 carrot, chopped
1 stalk celery, chopped
1 pound mushrooms, sliced
1 onion, minced
2 cloves garlic, minced
1 tablespoon dried basil
1 teaspoon dried oregano
2 basil leaves
1 cup macaroni
Salt and pepper to taste
½ cup Parmesan cheese

1. Combine the egg and milk in a medium-size bowl and stir until well mixed. Add the breadcrumbs and mix again. Add the ground beef and parsley and mix well with your hands. Shape into balls one inch in diameter and set aside.
2. In a large soup pot, combine the beef broth, tomatoes, cabbage, carrot, celery, mushrooms, onion, garlic, basil, oregano, and basil leaves and bring to a boil.

3. Add the macaroni and stir well. Cook the soup for 5 minutes. Add the meatballs, stir gently, and bring back to a low boil. Cook for 7 minutes or until the macaroni and meatballs are done. Add salt and pepper to taste.
4. Sprinkle Parmesan cheese on top and serve.

Cold Cucumber Soup

This might be an unusual meal for a book geared toward children, but my son loved this soup from the time he was very young, which is why I offer it to you. A quick, cold soup is wonderful for hot days when you don't want to heat up your kitchen. Serves 4.

2 cucumbers, peeled
1 scallion, equal parts white and green
1½ cups low-fat yogurt
¼ snipped fresh dill
¼ cup chopped fresh parsley
Salt, pepper, and paprika

1. Set aside half of one cucumber and half the scallion.
2. Chop the remaining cucumber into chunks.
3. Put the chopped cucumber, scallion, yogurt, dill, and parsley in blender and blend until smooth. Pour the soup into a bowl.
4. Finely chop the reserved cucumber. Mince the scallion.
5. Add the cucumber and scallion to the blended soup and mix. Add salt, pepper, and paprika to taste. Chill until serving time.
6. Pour into a chilled thermos for lunch.

Winter Soup

This is a generic recipe that you can adapt in lots of different ways. You can vary the broth, the meat, and the vegetables almost endlessly.

The method described here for thickening the broth also works well for making thick sauces and gravy. What I like about it is that it does not require additional fat and it always produces a perfectly smooth result.

If you have no broth, you can always use instant vegetable broth or bouillon cubes. Serves 2.

2 cups broth
2 tablespoons flour
1 cup cooked mixed vegetables such as carrots, celery, and onions
1 cup cut-up cooked chicken
2 tablespoons snipped fresh dill

1. Heat 1 cup of broth in a saucepan to boiling.
2. Meanwhile, pour the second cup of broth and the flour into the blender and blend until smooth.
3. When the broth is boiling, whirl the blender one more time, to make sure all the flour is really mixed well, and pour all at once into the boiling mixture. Immediately start stirring until the mixture comes back to a boil. Turn down the heat and let the mixture simmer for about 5 minutes, stirring occasionally, so that the flour is properly cooked through.
4. Add the vegetables and chicken, heat through, and adjust the seasoning.
5. Sprinkle the dill on top and serve hot.

Variations

- You can replace the second cup of broth with milk or cream for a creamy soup. Be sure to adjust the seasoning in the end, though, because the milk or cream is not salty and will make the soup blander.
- If you like your soup thicker, increase the flour to 3 tablespoons. Make notes to yourself in the margin of this recipe to remind yourself of how you like the result of your experiments.

- Some other cooked vegetables to add singly or in combination include cauliflower, broccoli, cooked sweet potato, beans, peas—whatever you like.
- You can include some proteins, too, such as cut-up beef, chicken, turkey, ham, sausage, or fish. Just be sure to adjust the broth to match the protein (not that hard: does beef broth, peas, and sole sound right to you?).

Potato Leek Soup or Light Vichyssoise

People make a big deal out of this soup, but in this child-friendly version, it is simplicity itself. The only "work" is washing the leeks, which has to be done thoroughly to make sure all the grit and sand are removed.

Taste the soup before adding salt; you might need more depending on how salty the broth is. You can make a vegetarian version by substituting vegetable broth for the chicken broth. Serves 4.

2 medium leeks
2 medium potatoes
4 cups chicken broth
½ teaspoon salt, or to taste

1. Use the white part of the leek and the soft green part. Cut the leek in 1-inch pieces and wash very well, to remove all the grit. You should have about 2 cups.
2. Peel and cube the potatoes. You should have about 3 cups.
3. Put the leeks, potatoes, and broth in a medium saucepan and bring to a boil. Simmer until the potatoes are very soft, about 15 to 20 minutes. Cool slightly.
4. Pour the soup into a blender and blend until the soup is completely smooth. Taste the soup and add salt to taste.

Dinners to Lunches

The real trick about making nutritious, fast lunches is planning ahead. Making a dinner that automatically supplies you with a lunch or two is a good way to do that. To some extent the idea here is that if you more or less cook for an army at home, you can eat like a king on the road. No one would make a pan of lasagna just for one lunch, but reheated lasagna at lunchtime is a luxurious treat.

I have collected some great basic recipes here, but as you go along I am sure you will find others. When you do, make a note of them here, so you won't forget. I have often "forgotten" good food ideas and "rediscovered" them, sometimes years later!

Barbecued Pot Roast

If your family loves pot roast, you might want to reserve a portion for sandwiches tomorrow before you serve it up. Otherwise it just might disappear at the dinner table! Serves 4.

4 pounds pot roast
½ teaspoon olive oil
1½ cups tomato sauce
1½ tablespoons Worcestershire sauce
1 tablespoon lemon juice
1 teaspoon brown sugar
1 cup finely chopped onions
8 carrots, scraped and cut into 1-inch sections
4 medium potatoes, scrubbed and cut into 1½-inch chunks
4 celery stalks, washed and cut into 1-inch sections

1. Preheat the oven to 350° F.
2. In a Dutch oven or large frying pan, heat the olive oil and brown the roast on all sides. Place the roast in a roasting pan.
3. In a separate bowl mix the tomato sauce, Worcestershire sauce, lemon juice, and brown sugar. Pour the sauce over the meat. Sprinkle the onions over all. Arrange the remaining vegetables around the beef. Cover tightly with aluminum foil and place in oven. Bake for 2½ hours or until the vegetables are done and the beef is tender.
4. Have the roast beef for dinner and reserve the leftover meat for sanwiches for lunch.

Chili

Little mouths can be sensitive to heat, so adjust the amount of chili powder according to your family's tastes. Once you have a teenager or two in the house, you might like to make lots of chili so you can feed them and their friends as well. Serve this with corn chips and chopped tomatoes on top. Serves 4 to 6.

1½ tablespoons olive oil
1 medium onion, chopped
1 green pepper, chopped
1 clove garlic, minced
1 pound ground beef
2 tablespoons chili powder
1½ teaspoons cumin powder
1½ teaspoons dried oregano
2 cups spaghetti sauce
16-ounce can kidney beans

1. In a large frying pan, heat the olive oil and sauté the onions and peppers on medium heat until the onions are transparent. Clear a space in the middle of the pan and add the garlic. Sauté the garlic for 20 seconds. Transfer the mixture to a large pot.
2. In the same pan brown the ground beef, breaking it up with the back of a spoon. Add a little more olive oil if you need it (it will depend on how lean the ground beef is). When the beef is browned, pour off the fat and add the beef to the pot with the onion mixture.
3. Add the rest of the ingredients and bring to a simmer. Simmer the chili for 20 minutes. Serve hot.
4. For lunch, pack some chili, reheated, in a thermos. Freeze leftovers.

Beef Stew

The secret of a good stew is browning the meat cubes a few at a time. This is the step most people skimp on, and it ruins the stew beyond hope from the start. Let me try to explain why this is so. The moment the cold cubes hit the pan, the pan cools down. If too much meat is browned at the same time, the pan cools down so much that none of the meat really sears, and this is the process that creates the flavor. So be patient, take your time browning the beef, and be rewarded with a fabulous stew.

Don't worry about using wine in this dish. The alcohol is burned off long before the dish is served, and only the taste stays behind. Serves 4.

- 1 to 1½ pounds beef stew meat cut in 1-inch cubes
- 1 tablespoon whole wheat flour
- ½ teaspoon salt
- Pepper
- ½ teaspoon dried thyme
- 1 tablespoon oil
- 1 cup chopped onions
- 1 cup red wine
- 1 cup water
- 1½ teaspoons Worcestershire sauce
- 2 celery stalks, cut in 1-inch chunks (1½ cups)
- 2 carrots, cut in medallions (1½ cups)
- 1 sweet potato, cut in 1-inch cubes (2 cups)

1. Put the beef stew meat in a bowl, sprinkle it with the flour, salt, pepper, and thyme, and mix well.
2. In a frying pan heat the oil and brown the meat a few cubes at a time. As the pieces of beef brown, transfer them to a large stove-top casserole.
3. In the same frying pan, fry the onions until they are translucent and starting to brown. Add the onions to the meat in the casserole.
4. Pour the wine, water, and Worcestershire sauce into the frying pan and bring it to boil, scraping the brown pieces from the bottom. Pour the liquid into the casserole. Mix well.

5. Bring the meat mixture to a boil, cover, and turn down the heat to low. Simmer for 1½ hours.
6. Add the celery, carrots, and sweet potato. Cover and simmer for 1 hour, stirring occasionally (the vegetables might sit on top of the liquid, but will steam to perfection). Serve hot.
7. Use leftover stew for lunch. Just reheat and spoon into a thermos.

Variations

- Substitute white potatoes for the sweet potatoes.
- Substitute other vegetables for the celery and carrots. Fennel, turnips, or green peppers are good choices.

Meatballs in Marinara Sauce

The jars of marinara sauce you find on your supermarket's shelves are perfectly fine. As a hassled parent, there is no way I am going to make that sauce from scratch for a regular family meal. Read the sauce jar labels, though, and make sure there is no added sugar in the form of corn syrup. Serves 3 to 4.

½ slice bread
⅓ cup coarsely chopped onions
1 egg
1 teaspoon tamari
½ teaspoon dried basil
½ pound ground beef
1 tablespoon olive oil
2 cups marinara sauce

1. Put the bread in a food processor fitted with the steel blade. Process until it turns into fine crumbs. Add the onions and process until the onion is completely blended with the bread.
2. Add the egg, tamari, and basil. Process until well blended. Add the ground beef and process until well blended.
3. In a large frying pan, heat the oil. In the meantime, make 12 large or 18 small meatballs and brown them.
4. Heat the marinara sauce in a saucepan and bring it to a simmer. Gently place the browned meatballs into the sauce and simmer for about 30 minutes.
5. For lunch, pack warmed-over pasta, sauce, and meatballs into a thermos. Freeze leftovers.

Meatloaf

This food processor technique allows you to get the meatloaf into the oven in a matter of minutes. The advantage of baking meatloaf in a non-traditional brownie pan is that you automatically have flat pieces of meatloaf that will fit perfectly on a piece of bread for a sandwich. This recipe is easily doubled (bake it in a loaf pan, for one hour). And if you are really organized, make an extra one and freeze it, for the next time. Serves 4 to 6.

2 slices bread
1 egg
¼ cup ketchup
1 teaspoon Worcestershire sauce
1 teaspoon dried oregano
1 pound ground beef

1. Preheat the oven to 350° F.
2. Put the bread slices in a food processor fitted with the steel blade. Process until they turn into fine crumbs.
3. Add the egg, ketchup, Worcestershire sauce, and oregano and process until well blended.
4. Add the ground beef and process until all is well blended.
5. Put the beef mixture into a 9-inch-square baking pan and smooth it out. Bake for 30 minutes.
6. Serve hot for dinner or at room temperature in a sandwich.

Garlic Roasted Chicken

If your oven has the space, never make fewer than two Garlic Roasted Chickens for dinner, but this recipe is for one. Any leftover bones after dinner, combined with the roasted giblets and onions, are excellent for making chicken soup or stock. The second chicken will provide plenty of meat for lunches for the week ahead (and the bones of this chicken ought to go into the soup pot, too!).

Chickens come in various weights, and ovens heat differently, so roasting times are always approximate. (Check the label on the bag the chicken was packaged in.) To make sure the chicken is done, juices must run clear when you pierce the chicken with a fork close to the bone, and there should be no red color on the bones.

Don't let chicken stand around at room temperature too long after the meal. Prepare the chicken right away for the next meal or put it into the refrigerator. Serves 6.

1 4-pound roasting chicken, fully defrosted if previously frozen
5 whole garlic cloves, peeled, crushed, and cut in quarters
1 lemon
1 teaspoon dried thyme
Salt and pepper to taste
1 cup coarsely chopped onions
1 teaspoon olive oil
Salt and pepper to taste

1. Preheat the oven to 350° F. Place a rack in a roasting pan. Remove the giblets from the cavity of the chicken and set aside for roasting separately.
2. Wash the chicken thoroughly with water. Dry the chicken with paper towels and place it, breast side up, on the rack set into the roasting pan. Pour enough water into the pan to cover the bottom.
3. Place the garlic cloves in the cavity. Wash the whole lemon thoroughly and cut off a third of it (reserve the rest of the lemon for another use). Squeeze some of the lemon juice over the chicken and place the lemon, peel and all, into the cavity.

4. Sprinkle thyme, salt, and pepper into the cavity and over the chicken. Tuck the wings close to the breast.
5. Put the chicken into the oven and bake until done. If the top of the chicken browns too quickly, place a loose aluminum foil tent over the breast.
6. Wash and dry the giblets. In a bowl combine the giblets, onion, and oil. Put the mixture in a small ovenproof dish and roast it alongside the chicken for 30 minutes or until the onions start to brown. Remove from oven and cool. Refrigerate it until you are ready to make chicken stock or soup.

Crispy Oven-Baked Chicken

Marinating chicken in buttermilk or yogurt is a fabulous way to tenderize it. Add some salt and pepper to the breadcrumbs in this recipe if you like. Makes 6 pieces.

2 chicken breasts (1 pound), each cut into thirds
1 cup buttermilk, or ½ cup plain yogurt mixed with ½ cup water
1½ teaspoons dried oregano
1 teaspoon dried basil
½ teaspoon dried thyme
1 to 2 cups seasoned breadcrumbs

1. Wash the chicken thoroughly with water. Pat dry with paper towels.
2. In a large bowl combine the buttermilk or yogurt and water mixture, oregano, basil, and thyme. Add the pieces of chicken and cover. Marinate for 2 to 4 hours, turning the pieces once in a while.
3. Preheat the oven to 350° F.
4. Place the breadcrumbs in a shallow bowl. One piece at a time, take the chicken out of the marinade and roll it in the breadcrumbs, covering the piece completely. Place the pieces meat-side up in a baking dish.
5. Bake the chicken for 40 minutes or until done. Serve immediately hot, or cool and serve at room temperature.

Honey-Mustard Chicken

This chicken is very flavorful and will work well for lunch in a chicken salad, sliced thinly in a sandwich, or on top of a Caesar salad. If you want to make this dish with a quartered chicken, just look in an all-purpose cookbook to adjust the cooking times. Serves 4 for dinner and 2 more for lunch.

¼ cup honey
¼ cup Dijon mustard
1 teaspoon dried basil
6 skinless chicken breasts

1. Preheat oven to 350° F. Line a baking dish with aluminum foil (for easy cleanup).
2. In a small bowl combine the honey, mustard, and basil. Brush the sauce over the entire breasts, and place them in the prepared pan.
3. Bake the chicken for 30 minutes, or until the chicken is cooked through. Serve hot for dinner. Cool the leftovers, cover, and refrigerate.

Double Shortcut Lasagna

A super easy lasagna with two timesaving shortcuts. First of all you don't have to cook the noodles separately and handle limp lasagna, because the baking time cooks the noodles. The second shortcut came about because I was just not in the mood to chop more vegetables. So I put the onion, celery stalks, and garlic cloves in the food processor and chopped them all in seconds flat!

I like my lasagna without meat, but if your family likes it with meat, feel free to add a pound of cooked ground beef to the pasta sauce. The alcohol in the wine is boiled off, so this recipe is perfectly suitable for children.

Assembling lasagna is a fun project to do with a child who has extremely clean hands. Think of it as a slightly messy art or building project.

Since lasagna freezes so well, make a second one at the same time and give yourself an easy meal some other time. Makes 15 pieces.

1 26-ounce jar pasta sauce
1 cup water
1 cup red wine
1 onion, peeled and cut in large chunks
1 stalk celery, cut in large chunks
3 cloves garlic, peeled and cut in quarters
1½ teaspoons dried oregano
1 pound part-skim mozzarella
2 eggs
1 10-ounce package frozen spinach, cooked according to package directions and squeezed dry
3 cups part-skim ricotta cheese
Salt and pepper to taste
½ cup grated Parmesan cheese
1 pound uncooked lasagna noodles

1. Preheat the oven to 350° F.
2. In a large mixing bowl, combine the pasta sauce, water, and wine and mix well. Set aside.

3. In a food processor fitted with the steel blade, pour one cup of the tomato and wine sauce and add the onion, celery, garlic, and oregano. Pulse the processor on and off, scraping down the sides a few times, until the vegetables are in uniform little pieces. Do not process until all the vegetables are liquefied. Add the onion mixture to the reserved pasta and wine sauce and blend well.
4. Change the blade in the processor to a coarse grind and grate the mozzarella. Set the mozzarella aside in a bowl.
5. In a large bowl beat the eggs well. Add the spinach and ricotta and mix well. Season with salt and pepper if desired.
6. It is now time to assemble the lasagna; the only trick is to distribute the ingredients evenly over the entire surface. Pour a cup of the tomato sauce in the bottom of a 9-by-13-inch baking dish. On top of that place a layer of uncooked lasagna noodles. Pour a cup of tomato sauce over the noodles, then a third of the ricotta mix, then a third of the mozzarella. Repeat this twice more: noodles, sauce, ricotta, and mozzarella.
7. Finish with a final layer of noodles and pour the remaining sauce evenly over all. Sprinkle the top with the Parmesan cheese. The lasagna should not reach to the top of the pan because the noodles will expand a bit as they cook.
8. Cover the pan tightly with aluminum foil and bake for 1 hour.
9. Remove the foil and continue baking, uncovered, for 15 minutes, or until the noodles are soft in the center (a knife should go in easily, but be sure you do not pierce the bottom of the pan if it is aluminum).
10. Let the lasagna rest for 10 minutes before serving.
11. Freeze leftover portions in serving sizes. For lunch, reheat the lasagna and pack it in a thermos.

Poached Salmon

Easy, fast, delicious, healthy, and leftovers make a great lunch salad. Salmon might very well be the first fish your children like because of its mild taste. Don't worry about cooking with wine; the alcohol evaporates in the first few minutes of simmering. Serves 4.

1½ teaspoons olive oil
3 scallions, white and 3 inches of green, minced
1 cup white wine
1½ pounds salmon fillet
Salt and pepper
1 tablespoon sour cream
1 tablespoon snipped fresh dill

1. In a frying pan heat the oil briefly. Add the scallions and fry them for a minute.
2. Pour in the wine. Add the salmon and sprinkle with salt and pepper. Heat the wine slowly, but do not let it come to a boil. Cover the pan.
3. Simmer just below boiling until the salmon is cooked through (this will depend entirely on how thick the fillet is).
4. Remove the salmon to a warm serving plate. Add the sour cream to the poaching liquid, heat through without coming to a boil, and pour over the salmon. Sprinkle dill on top.
5. Serve with steamed red potatoes and baby carrots. Leftover salmon can be used to make salmon salad (see Sandwiches chapter).

Brown Rice

Having cooked brown rice on hand is a good kitchen strategy for so many reasons. You can whip up a stir-fry in minutes, a rice salad for lunch is a few chopped ingredients away, and a classic and nourishing rice pudding is right around the corner. If you are going to watch some TV anyway, just put up a quick pot of rice, set the timer, and at the end of the show your rice is done. Makes 2 cups.

1 cup brown rice

2 cups water

1. Put the rice and water in a pot and bring it to a boil. Stir, cover, and turn down the heat.
2. Simmer for 50 minutes.
3. Serve for dinner, refrigerate leftovers, or freeze serving-size portions of cooled-down rice.

Parsley Potatoes

Having cooked potatoes in the refrigerator is like having a spare $20 bill tucked in the back of your wallet: It gives you a little bit of extra confidence. You are minutes away from a nourishing meal of home fries, potato salad, or potato soup. If you put up the potatoes before you clean up after the night's meal, they will be cooked through by the time you are done wiping the counters. Makes 3 cups.

10 new potatoes

¼ cup minced fresh parsley

1. Bring water to a boil in a saucepan.
2. Wash the potatoes and half or quarter them. Carefully place the potatoes in the water (so the hot water doesn't splash you) and boil them until they are soft when pierced with a fork. Depending on the size of the potato pieces, this may take from fifteen to thirty minutes.
3. Drain the potatoes, sprinkle with parsley, and serve hot.
4. Use leftover potatoes for potato salad and other meals.

Baked Goodies and Other Snacks

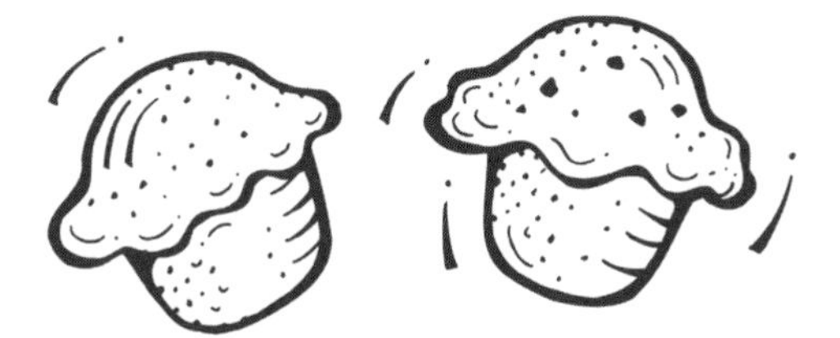

The most challenging part of a healthy lunch is the snack. Out in the marketplace, snacks are made to appeal to our taste buds, but not to add any nutrition. Lunch is too important a meal to fill it up with empty calories, so this is an issue worth paying attention to.

I have used both brown and white sugar, honey, and maple sugar as sweeteners, and I have used them in moderation, so far as possible. If your child is seriously obese or diabetic, these will not all be appropriate recipes for you and you will have to use your judgment. The best way to deal with the inevitable spike that comes with sugar is to make sure that it is consumed with some protein. Also, try to use snacks that have the lowest sugar content.

Some of the snacks in this chapter are nutritious enough that they are also suitable for an occasional breakfast, such as Carole's Muffins and the Peanut Butter Granola Bars. And if your child is on a very early school bus and the wait for lunch is especially long, or if lunchtime is especially late, having a little snack for him or her to eat between classes might be a good idea.

The key to giving your children snacks is a combination of moderation, good judgment, and the cooperation of your children, which you can only get with enough education. Help them make the connection between good nutrition and feeling and looking good, and they will understand that treats are never a substitute for healthy, nourishing food.

Have fun with some of the recipes here. They are quick and easy, produce a great result, and are worth it as an occasional treat.

Baking with Confidence

Baking is not hard. Here are a few tips that will add both taste and nutrition to your baking.

Be sure that there are no clumps in the baking soda or baking powder. Sift to be certain.

Use rolled oats whenever possible because they are heart healthy. Don't use the quick-cooking kinds.

You can use whole wheat flour in most recipes, but sometimes it makes the finished product too dense. When you do use white flour, be sure to use flour that is not bleached.

Use light brown sugar, which works particularly well with whole wheat flour. It also imparts a nice flavor.

When you are looking for recipes to add to your healthy snack collection, try other flours, such as buckwheat flour or millet flour, but don't substitute at random. Flours have different properties. Look for specific recipes that are developed for these flours.

I use sweet (unsalted) butter because I don't like the added salt. (The salt also tends to mask the flavor of the butter, and you would be more likely to eat rancid butter because you could not properly taste it!) If your doctor forbids it, you'll need to change to margarine, but I would rather eat a little of a natural product than some chemical combination that has a vague resemblance to the original product.

Banana Muffins

I like muffins because they are such handy little packages, so I adapted my banana bread recipe to make muffins instead. Overripe bananas are often available—and cheap—so pick some up when they are on sale in the supermarket. Peel them and freeze them in plastic bags. They will turn dark when frozen, but that will make no difference to the final result. You can also use them right away and have extra muffins to freeze. Makes 9 muffins.

3 ripe bananas, cut in pieces
¼ cup honey
½ cup unsalted butter, cut in pieces
1 egg
1½ teaspoons vanilla extract
1½ cups whole wheat flour
2 teaspoons baking powder

1. Preheat the oven to 375° F. Spray a muffin pan with vegetable spray, or place nine baking cups in the muffin pan.
2. Put the bananas, honey, butter, egg, and extract in a food processor fitted with the steel blade. Blend well. Add the flour and baking powder. Blend until mixed.
3. Spoon the batter into 9 muffin cups. Bake for 30 minutes or until a wooden toothpick inserted into the middle of a muffin comes out clean.
4. Let the muffins cool in the pan for a few minutes. Then remove them from the pan and let cool completely.

Carole's Muffins

These might well become your favorite muffins because there is nothing but healthy ingredients in them. They are perfect for both breakfast and lunch, and you can make them in 5 minutes flat! Do like my friend Carole Owens does and line up all the ingredients first. Then put each one away as you use it. That way you will never forget to put anything in. For very small children, you might want to omit the nuts because they could be a choking hazard. Makes 12 muffins.

2 cups rolled oats
1 cup whole wheat flour
¼ teaspoon salt
½ teaspoon ground cinnamon
1 tablespoon baking powder
⅓ cup water
1 egg
½ cup extra-light-tasting olive oil
½ cup maple syrup
½ cup walnuts
½ cup raisins

1. Preheat the oven to 350° F. Spray a muffin pan with vegetable spray, or place baking cups in the muffin pan.
2. Pour the oats into a food processor fitted with the steel blade. With on/off pulses cut the oat flakes into small pieces. It is not necessary to grind the oats to flour.
3. Add the whole wheat flour, salt, cinnamon, and baking powder and mix. Add the water and the egg. Mix well. Add the oil and syrup and blend until well mixed. Add the walnuts and mix with little on/off pulses.
4. Add the raisins and mix lightly with a spoon (don't run the machine).
5. With the spoon divide the batter among the muffin cups. Bake for 20 minutes or until a wooden toothpick inserted in the middle of a muffin comes out clean.
6. Let the muffins cool in the pan for a few minutes. Then remove them from the pan and let cool completely.

Apple, Oatmeal, and Coconut Muffins

Not too sweet and packed with nutrients, these muffins will do equally well for breakfast as for a lunch treat.

You may leave the peel on the apples if your child doesn't mind. Makes 12 muffins.

2 cups chopped apples
1 cup rolled oats
1 cup low-fat plain yogurt
⅔ cup honey
⅓ cup shredded unsweetened coconut
⅓ cup extra-light-tasting olive oil
1 egg
1½ cups whole wheat flour
2 teaspoons baking powder
2 teaspoons ground cinnamon
¼ teaspoon ground cloves

1. Preheat the oven to 375° F. Spray a muffin pan with vegetable spray, or place baking cups in the muffin pan.
2. In a mixing bowl, combine the apples, oats, yogurt, honey, coconut, and oil. Mix well. Let the mixture stand for 10 minutes.
3. Add the egg and mix thoroughly.
4. In another mixing bowl combine the flour, baking powder, and spices and mix well. Add to the oat mixture and stir until the dry ingredients are moistened.
5. Fill the muffin cups; they will be quite full. Bake for 25 minutes or until a wooden toothpick inserted into the middle of a muffin comes out clean.
6. Let the muffins cool in the pan for a few minutes. Then remove them from the pan and let cool completely.

Squash Corn Muffins

This is one of the recipes where you can sneak some vegetables in a place where your child might not be aware of it! It is a perfect way to use up a little leftover squash at the end of a meal. I used some white flour here because the results with all whole wheat flour were a little too dense. Makes 12 muffins.

¾ cup cornmeal
¾ cup whole wheat flour
½ cup unbleached all-purpose flour
2½ tablespoons dry buttermilk powder
1 tablespoon baking powder
½ teaspoon salt
½ teaspoon ground cinnamon
¼ teaspoon ground cloves
⅔ cup light brown sugar
¼ cup unsalted butter, cut in pieces
2 eggs
2 tablespoons honey
¾ cup pureed cooked squash (or pumpkin)
⅔ cup water

1. Preheat the oven to 350° F. Spray a muffin pan with vegetable spray, or place baking cups in the muffin pan.
2. In a large bowl combine the cornmeal, whole wheat flour, white flour, buttermilk powder, baking powder, salt, cinnamon, and cloves. Mix well.
3. Pour the sugar, butter, eggs, and honey in a food processor fitted with the steel blade. Blend until smooth. Add the squash and water and mix well.
4. Add the squash mixture to the flour mixture and blend well with a long-handled spoon.
5. Spoon the batter evenly into the 12 muffin cups and bake for 20 minutes, or until a wooden toothpick inserted into the middle of a muffin comes out clean.
6. Let the muffins cool in the pan for a few minutes. Then remove them from the pan and let cool completely.

Corn Muffins

These muffins are much less sweet than the commercial ones. With a little butter and jam, they will be sweet enough. As with most muffins, they are good to grab when there is too little time for breakfast. Makes 12 muffins.

1 cup unbleached all-purpose flour
1 cup whole wheat flour
1 cup cornmeal
1 tablespoon baking powder
¼ teaspoon salt
1½ cups milk
⅓ cup extra-light-tasting olive oil
¼ cup light brown sugar
1 egg

1. Preheat the oven to 375° F. Spray a muffin pan with vegetable spray, or place baking cups in the muffin pan.
2. In a large bowl mix the flours, cornmeal, baking powder, and salt.
3. In a medium bowl mix the milk, oil, sugar, and egg.
4. Add the liquid ingredients to the dry ingredients and mix.
5. Spoon the batter evenly into the muffin tins. Bake for 30 minutes or until a wooden toothpick inserted into the center of a muffin comes out clean.
6. Let the muffins cool in the pan for a few minutes. Then remove them from the pan and let cool completely.

Date and Sour Cream Muffins

These muffins are so delicious you won't need any butter or jam on them. If your child is old enough to handle a knife, teach him how to cut up the dates. Make 12 muffins.

1 cup dates
1 cup unbleached all-purpose flour
½ cup whole wheat flour
1 teaspoon baking powder
1 cup light brown sugar
1 stick unsalted butter, cut into pieces
2 eggs
1 cup reduced-fat sour cream
1 teaspoon vanilla extract

1. Preheat the oven to 325° F. Spray a muffin pan with vegetable spray, or place baking cups in the muffin pan.
2. Cut the dates into small pieces the size of raisins and set aside.
3. In a large bowl mix the flours and baking powder.
4. Combine the brown sugar and butter in a food processor fitted with the steel blade and process until well mixed. Add the eggs, sour cream and vanilla, and the flour mixture, processing after each addition until well blended. Scrape down the sides, add the dates, and process again until just mixed.
5. Spoon the batter into the baking cups. Bake for 20 to 25 minutes or until a wooden toothpick inserted into the middle of a muffin comes out clean.
6. Let the muffins cool in the pan for a few minutes. Then remove them from the pan and let cool completely.

Orange and Carrot Muffins

Two different fruits and a vegetable fill this muffin with nutrition and goodness. From vitamins to fiber, it's all in here, and it's good for breakfast, too. If your family doesn't like prunes, you can use raisins instead. Makes 12 muffins.

1 cup grated carrots
1 banana, mashed
½ cup cut-up prunes
2 eggs
⅓ cup extra-light-tasting olive oil
⅓ cup honey
1 cup orange juice
1 teaspoon orange extract
2 cups whole wheat flour
¼ cup oat bran
2 teaspoons baking powder

1. Preheat the oven to 375° F. Spray a muffin pan with vegetable spray, or place baking cups in the muffin pan.
2. In a large mixing bowl, place the grated carrots, banana, and prunes. Mix well.
3. Add the eggs, oil, and honey. Mix well.
4. Add the juice and orange extract. Mix well.
5. In a separate bowl combine the flour, bran, and baking powder. Mix well. Add to the carrot mixture and blend together until the dry ingredients are moistened.
6. Divide the batter evenly among the 12 muffin cups. Bake for 25 minutes.
7. Let the muffins cool in the pan for a few minutes. Then remove them from the pan and let cool completely.

Cheesecake Muffins

There are decisions I make while developing recipes that sometimes are due to the fact that I have unexpectedly run out of an ingredient. Making the bottom "crust" out of crushed cereal in this recipe happened because I didn't realize I had run out of graham crackers. I liked the result so much that I decided to include it. The loose crumbs will probably float up a little when you pour the batter into the muffin pan. So what, it's just a little snack! If it bothers you, by all means find a "real" crust recipe and make it from scratch.

Use the block-style cream cheese, not the whipped kind. I use whole wheat flour out of habit, but if you want the cheesecake to be more snowy white, use white flour. Makes 12 muffins.

¾ cup crushed cereal or graham crackers
1½ cups low-fat cottage cheese
8 ounces reduced-fat cream cheese, cut in pieces
1 cup white sugar
3 eggs
¼ cup low-fat sour cream
1 teaspoon vanilla extract
1 teaspoon grated lemon rind
3 tablespoons flour

1. Preheat the oven to 325° F. Spray a muffin pan with vegetable spray, or place baking cups in the muffin pan.
2. Put 1 tablespoon of crushed cereal or cracker crumbs in the bottom of each muffin cup. Set aside.
3. Put the cottage cheese in a food processor fitted with the steel blade and process until very smooth. Add the cream cheese and sugar and process, again, until very smooth. Scrape down the sides making sure all is well blended.
4. Add the eggs, sour cream, vanilla extract, and lemon rind and process until smooth. Add the flour and process until smooth.
5. Pour the very liquid batter into the prepared tins. Bake for 35 minutes. Turn off the oven and let the cheesecake muffins remain in the closed oven for 20 minutes longer.
6. Remove the pan from the oven and let cool completely.

Peanut Butter Granola Bars

I shudder when I look at the ingredient list for some of the commercial granola bars. Don't assume that these products are "health" food. And be especially aware of all the hidden sugars. Sometimes there are as many as three different kinds of sugars, and though sugar does not show up as a single main ingredient, added together, they dominate! Makes 10 bars.

1½ cups rolled oats
½ cup oat bran
¼ cup dry nonfat milk powder
½ cup raisins
⅓ cup honey
¼ cup peanut butter
¼ cup extra-light-tasting olive oil
½ teaspoon vanilla extract
1 egg

1. Preheat oven to 350° F. Lightly grease a 9-inch-square pan.
2. In a large bowl mix the oats, oat bran, and dry milk. Add the raisins and mix well again, making sure the raisins are separated.
3. In a small saucepan combine the honey, peanut butter, oil, and extract. Over very low heat, stir the honey mixture well for a few moments. Do *not* let the mixture get hot; you only want to raise the heat a little so that the ingredients will combine easily. Take the saucepan off the heat, add the egg, and mix well.
4. Pour the honey mixture over the oat mixture, and with a wooden spoon blend well until all the dry ingredients are moistened.
5. Pour the oat mixture into the prepared pan and distribute the mixture somewhat evenly. Bake the granola bars for 20 minutes.
6. Score into bars with the edge of a spatula. Let the bars cool in the pan, then invert them onto a plate and cut through to separate the bars. Store in an airtight container.

Variation

- Instead of peanut butter, use a different butter such as almond butter. If you use almond butter, substitute almond extract for the vanilla extract.

Carrot Blondies

Most carrot cakes have just a token amount of carrots in them, but not this one. You'll find lots of orange shards bursting with vitamin A in every bite. This cake comes out flat like pan brownies. I like it best split open like a scone with some cream cheese in the middle. Makes 18 blondies.

2 eggs
½ cup extra-light-tasting olive oil
½ cup honey
½ teaspoon ground cinnamon
⅔ cup whole wheat flour
⅔ cup unbleached all-purpose flour
2 teaspoons baking powder
2 cups shredded carrots (approximately 3 carrots)

1. Preheat the oven to 350° F. Grease and flour a 9-by-13-inch pan.
2. Put the eggs in a food processor fitted with the steel blade and blend. Add the oil and honey and process until well blended. Add the cinnamon, flours, and baking powder and blend.
3. Place the flour mixture in a large bowl. Add the carrots and mix well.
4. Pour the mixture in the baking pan and spread out gently. Bake for 25 minutes or until a wooden toothpick inserted in the middle of the cake comes out clean. Let cool in the pan before cutting into squares.

Peanut Butter Bars

These peanut butter bars are much better for you than the store-bought ones. Though not low in fat and calories, they are very filling, so a little goes a long way. Freeze these so that you'll have them on hand when your child needs a filling snack on a field trip or scout hike. Makes 12 bars.

⅔ cup light brown sugar
½ cup peanut butter, smooth or chunky
4 tablespoons unsalted butter, softened
2 eggs
1½ teaspoons vanilla extract
¾ cup whole wheat flour
1½ teaspoons baking powder

1. Preheat oven to 350° F. Grease a 9-inch-square pan.
2. Combine the sugar, peanut butter, butter, eggs, and vanilla in a food processor fitted with the steel blade. Blend until well mixed.
3. Add the flour and baking powder to the peanut butter mixture. Blend until well mixed. The dough will be stiff.
4. Scrape the dough into the prepared pan, and with a spatula carefully spread the dough out and smooth the top. Bake for 22 minutes, or until a toothpick inserted into the middle comes out clean.
5. Cut the cake into 12 bars. Let the cake cool for a few minutes, and then remove the bars. Let cool completely. Store in an airtight container.

Apricot Bars

These energy bars are easy to make and don't contain the added artificial ingredients that many of the commercial ones do. The apricots I used in this recipe were nice and plump. If you have apricots that are dry, plump them in hot water for thirty minutes, and dry them off before you use them. Be sure you buy dried fruit that has not been treated with sulfites. These bars will work for breakfast, as a lunch snack, or as a great part of your backpacking fare. Makes 24 bars.

1 cup dried apricots
1 cup rolled oats
½ cup sesame seeds
½ cup unsalted butter, slightly softened, cut in slices
1 cup light brown sugar
2 eggs
1 cup whole wheat flour
1 teaspoon baking powder
1 teaspoon ground cinnamon

1. Preheat the oven to 350° F. Grease a 9-by-13-inch baking pan.
2. Put the apricots and oats in a food processor fitted with the steel blade and process until the oats are cut into little ⅛-inch pieces. Put the apricot mixture into a bowl, add the sesame seeds, mix, and set aside.
3. Without washing the food processor bowl, process the butter and sugar until smooth. Add the eggs and process until smooth. Add the flour, baking powder, and cinnamon to the butter mixture and process until well mixed. Finally, add the apricot mixture and process, pulsing on and off, until well blended. The batter will be stiff.
4. Spread the batter into the prepared pan and smooth out without compressing too much. Bake for 25 minutes.
5. Let cool in pan for 5 minutes. Cut 24 bars, remove them from the pan, and let cool completely. Store in an airtight container in the refrigerator.

Variation

- Replace the apricots with equal amounts of other dried fruits.

Gorp

Gorp is a mixture of dried fruits, nuts, and other little snacks that backpackers take along to give them concentrated energy. Kids love this little treat, and you can easily make small bags filled with goodies to pack in their lunches. Pack small amounts of dried fruits and nuts and add some of the other ingredients listed here as a special treat. If your child is very young, you might not want to include the nuts just yet. Gorp looks especially nice if the ingredients are roughly the same size.

Your health food store is probably the best place to find fruit that is dried without sulfites or added sugar. It is also the best place to find nuts, which should always be refrigerated because the oil in them can go rancid quickly.

By the way, any one of these ingredients would make a fine little snack, too: popcorn with a sprinkle of Parmesan cheese, a baggie with dried apple slices, a few pretzels—all are great snacks for a busy mom or dad on the go to make.

Even a very young child can help to make these little bags of snacks. It's a good opportunity to practice counting skills (six pretzels in each bag), but be sure to do this project on a full stomach, otherwise the temptation to "sample the merchandise" will make too many of the ingredients disappear during the packing!

Dried fruit

Currants
Dried apples
Dried apricots
Dried banana chips
Dried blueberries
Dried cherries
Dried coconut pieces
Dried cranberries
Dried dates
Dried figs
Dried mangoes
Dried papayas
Dried pineapples
Raisins

Nuts

Almonds
Brazil nuts
Cashews
Chestnuts
Filberts
Macadamia nuts
Peanuts
Pecans
Pine nuts
Pistachios
Pumpkin seeds
Soy nuts
Sunflower seeds, hulled
Walnuts

Crunch

Crackers such as fishies and oyster crackers
Popcorn (hot-air popped)
Pretzels

Special treats

Animal crackers
Butterscotch chips
Carob chips
Cereal, such as Chex or Cheerios
Chocolate chips
Chocolate-covered raisins or almonds
M&Ms

Snack Balls

These will be popular with the younger crowd. They are a good "candy" to make when you're weaning your child from sugary sweets.

This is also a great food project to do with your children. If the peanut butter is soft and at room temperature, even very little hands can knead all the ingredients together. All in all it'll make for one of those good times when "playing with your food" is something you want to encourage! You can freeze Snack Balls to have on hand when you need them. Makes 5 to 10 balls.

½ cup dry nonfat milk powder
¼ cup oat bran
1 tablespoon ground cinnamon
⅛ teaspoon ground cloves
¼ cup honey
¼ cup peanut butter
2 tablespoons shredded coconut

1. In a mixing bowl combine the dried milk, bran, cinnamon, and cloves. Add the honey and peanut butter. Mix well.
2. Make gumball-to-walnut-size balls, rolling them between your palms (yeah, you can also make snakes!).
3. Place the coconut in a shallow bowl. Roll the balls in the coconut.

Variations

- You can add two tablespoons currants or raisins or other dried fruit, cut into small pieces.
- Try almond butter or other nut butters instead of peanut butter.

Fruit and Nut Energizers

These are high calorie and high energy and are great on a long hike or to still a hungry tummy before dinner. Use the nuts and fruits your family likes. You can store these in the freezer for a month or two. Makes 40 balls, depending on the size.

3 cups dried fruit such as apples, prunes, pears, raisins, figs, or dates
1 cup nuts, such as walnuts, pecans, or pumpkin seeds
1 tablespoon maple syrup
¼ teaspoon dried ground sweet spices, such as cinnamon, cloves, or cardamom
Shredded, unsweetened coconut

1. Put the dried fruit, nuts, maple syrup, and spices in a food processor fitted with the steel blade. Process until blended.
2. Roll the "dough" into balls and roll the balls in the coconut. Let them dry for an hour and then store in an airtight container.

Carole's Cookies

This is the best all-round, healthy, yummy, fast, and easy-to-make cookie, courtesy of my friend Carole Owens. The cookies are a variation on her muffin recipe at the beginning of the chapter. Carole always has a supply of cookies in the freezer, and she warms them up for me in the microwave for a few seconds. Her original version contains walnuts, which you might want to omit if your children are very young. Makes 12 cookies.

1 cup rolled oats (not instant)
1 cup whole wheat flour
1 cup walnuts
½ cup extra-light-tasting olive oil
½ cup maple syrup
Pinch of salt

1. Preheat the oven to 375° F. Take out a large cookie sheet.
2. Put the oats in a food processor fitted with a steel blade. Pulse on and off until the oatmeal is in small pieces. There will still be little pieces of oatmeal visible, and these will give the finished cookie a nice chewy texture.
3. Add the flour and process. Add the walnuts, oil, maple syrup, and salt and run the food processor until all is well mixed.
4. Drop the batter on the cookie sheet, a generous tablespoon per cookie. Bake for 12 minutes.
5. Remove the cookies and let them cool on a plate. Freeze leftovers. You can let the cookies thaw on their own, or warm them up in the microwave for a fresh-baked sensation.

Variation

- While the cookie is cooling, you can make a little well in the top by pushing a small teaspoon into the center. Fill the depression with a bit of all-fruit spread.

Soda Bread Scones

Scones are not just for the grown-ups to have with their lattes! These are light little buns, perfect for a snack or a special treat with apple butter or some butter and jam. Make these once and if you like them as much as my tasters did, premix the dry ingredients in plastic bags and freeze them. That way you only have to add shortening and a little water and you can have fresh scones in 35 minutes. Be sure to write the instructions on a piece of paper and include them on or in the bag.

Do not handle or knead the dough too much; the less you do the lighter and fluffier the rolls. Makes 6 scones.

1 cup unbleached all-purpose flour
1 cup whole wheat flour
2 tablespoons dry buttermilk powder
1 tablespoon light brown sugar
1½ teaspoons baking powder
½ teaspoon baking soda
½ teaspoon salt
4 tablespoons unsalted butter, cut into ½-teaspoon size pieces
¾ cup water

1. Preheat the oven to 375° F. Take out a nonstick cookie sheet.
2. Sift together the dry ingredients and pour into a food processor fitted with a steel blade.
3. Add the butter pieces and process about 10 seconds, or until the butter pieces are the size of a lentil.
4. Add the water all at once and process for a few seconds (don't try to get it all mixed perfectly). Turn the dough onto a board and quickly finish the mixing, without too much kneading.
5. Make 6 scones and place them on the nonstick cookie sheet. Bake the scones for 25 to 30 minutes.

Variation

- Add ½ cup currants, raisins, or other cut-up dried fruit when you add the water.

Sweet Potato Biscuits

Talk about a sneaky way to feed your child some vegetables! After you make all the biscuits, there will be a little dough left over. Perfect for a doll-size biscuit! Makes 12 to 16 biscuits.

1½ cups whole wheat flour
1 cup unbleached all-purpose flour
¼ cup unsalted butter, cut into little pieces
2 tablespoons dry buttermilk powder
4 teaspoons baking powder
1 teaspoon salt
1 cup cooked sweet potato
½ cup water
4 teaspoons honey
½ teaspoon orange extract

1. Preheat the oven to 400° F.
2. Combine the whole wheat flour, white flour, butter, buttermilk powder, and salt in a food processor fitted with the steel blade. Process until the butter is reduced to pea-size pieces. Pour the flour mixture into a large mixing bowl.
3. Without washing the bowl, put the sweet potato, water, honey, and orange extract into the food processor and blend until well mixed. Pour the sweet potato mixture into the flour mixture. Blend with two spoons and later with your hands until the dough holds together. It will seem as if there is not enough wet ingredient to moisten the flour, but trust me, there is.
4. Turn the dough onto a lightly floured board and roll out to about ¾ inch (or pat it flat with the heel of your hand). With an overturned glass, cut out the biscuits. Take the remaining dough, roll it out again, and make more biscuits, until all the dough is used up.
5. Place the biscuits on a nonstick cookie sheet and bake for 11 to 13 minutes, or until the biscuits are done.

Variation

- Try lemon extract for a refreshing difference.

Apple Squares

If you like these squares, you can mix a few batches of the dry ingredients and keep them, labeled, in the freezer. That way you are always just minutes away from a pan of delicious snacks.

Instead of the dry milk and water, you can add a little more than ⅔ cup milk. For variety, mix in other fruits as well; blueberries are particularly nice (omit the raisins). However, bringing blueberry desserts to school will leave your child with a stained mouth, a situation that might be anything from "cool" to embarrassing. Makes 18 squares.

½ cup whole wheat flour
½ cup unbleached all-purpose flour
½ cup light brown sugar
⅓ cup dry nonfat milk powder
1 teaspoon baking powder
¼ teaspoon ground cloves
Pinch salt
1 egg
⅔ cup water
3 medium apples, peeled and sliced
⅓ cup raisins
¼ cup light brown sugar
1 teaspoon ground cinnamon

1. Preheat the oven to 350° F. Grease a 13-by-9-inch pan and set aside.
2. In a large bowl combine the whole wheat flour, unbleached flour, ½ cup brown sugar, milk powder, baking powder, cloves, and salt and mix well.
3. In a small bowl mix the egg and water and add to the flour mixture. Blend well.
4. Pour the batter in the prepared pan and spread the batter evenly.
5. Place the apples over the batter (in rows or some other nice pattern) and sprinkle the raisins over the top. In a small bowl, mix the ¼ cup brown sugar and cinnamon. Sprinkle the sugar mixture over all.
6. Bake for 35 minutes or until a wooden toothpick inserted in the middle comes out clean.

Cranberry Bread

When cranberries are in the supermarket in the fall, I buy a few extra packages and freeze them so I can make cranberry bread and cranberry relish all year long. Cranberries are much too tart to eat raw, but in breads and muffins they give a nice tart bite that kids often like. Cranberries also provide valuable nutrients, so be sure to eat them once in a while. Makes 1 loaf.

2 eggs
¾ cup light brown sugar
¼ cup unsalted butter, softened
½ cup orange juice
1 teaspoon vanilla extract
1 teaspoon orange extract
2 cups whole wheat flour
2 teaspoons baking powder
1 tablespoon dry buttermilk powder
1½ cups cranberries, frozen or fresh, washed and picked over

1. Preheat the oven to 375° F. Grease a loaf pan.
2. Put the eggs and sugar in a food processor fitted with the steel blade. Process until well blended. Add the butter, orange juice, and extracts. Process until well mixed. Add the flour, baking powder, and buttermilk powder and process until just mixed.
3. Place the batter in a large bowl, add the cranberries, and mix well. Pour the batter into the prepared pan. Bake for 50 minutes, or until a toothpick inserted into the middle comes out clean.
4. Let the bread cool in the pan for 10 minutes before unmolding. Let cool completely.

Gingerbread

This bread does have some sugar in it, but as you can see, virtually no fat. If your children like this a lot, keep a jar with several loaves worth of spices premixed in it (just keep the 1–¼–¼ proportions), and after shaking the jar well, all you'll need to do is scoop out 1½ teaspoons. Makes 9 large pieces.

1½ cups whole wheat flour
⅔ cup light brown sugar
1 teaspoon baking soda
½ teaspoon baking powder
1 teaspoon ground ginger
¼ teaspoon ground cloves
¼ teaspoon ground cinnamon
2 eggs
⅓ cup applesauce
⅓ cup water
½ teaspoon apple cider vinegar

1. Preheat the oven to 300° F. Grease a 9-inch-square baking pan.
2. In a large bowl combine the flour, sugar, baking soda, baking powder, ginger, cloves, and cinnamon.
3. In a separate bowl combine the eggs, applesauce, water, and vinegar.
4. Add the liquid ingredients to the flour mixture and combine lightly but thoroughly. Pour the batter into the prepared pan and smooth out. Bake for 25 minutes or until a wooden toothpick inserted in the middle comes out clean.
5. Let the gingerbread cool in the pan for 10 minutes before unmolding it. Serve warm or cool.

One-Pan Cake

Once my kids learned to prepare this simple cake, we ate it often. It takes just minutes to make, and only one pan and a few measuring spoons and cups get dirty. The other advantage is that the ingredients are generally available in your home. I adapted the original recipe to make this cake a bit healthier. It's wonderful with a scoop of ice cream. Makes 1 cake.

1¼ cups whole wheat flour
1 cup light brown sugar
¼ cup oat bran
3 tablespoons cocoa powder
1 tablespoon dry nonfat milk powder
1 teaspoon baking soda
¼ teaspoon salt
6 tablespoons extra-light-tasting olive oil
1 tablespoon apple cider vinegar
1 teaspoon vanilla extract
1 cup low-fat milk or water

1. Preheat the oven to 350° F.
2. Mix the flour, sugar, bran, cocoa powder, milk powder, baking soda, and salt in an ungreased 9-inch-square pan. Make sure all the ingredients are well distributed.
3. Make three wells in the flour mixture. Pour the oil in one well, the vinegar in another, and the vanilla in the third. Pour the milk over all. Mix everything well. If you are using a nonstick pan you might want to mix with a plastic spoon so you don't gouge it.
4. Bake for 30 minutes or until a wooden toothpick inserted in the middle comes out clean.

Apple Pie-Cake

Here's one of those decidedly homespun cakes you would only serve to your family and friends—never in a fancy bake-off. Because this is such an easy dessert to make, it would be a perfect first cake for a child to learn how to bake.

You might not think there are enough wet ingredients in this recipe to make a batter, but it works surprisingly well. Serves 6.

1 egg
¾ cup light brown sugar
1½ teaspoons vanilla extract
4 apples, peeled, cored, and chopped
½ cup whole wheat flour
¼ teaspoon ground cinnamon
1 teaspoon baking powder
Pinch of salt

1. Preheat the oven to 350° F. Butter a pie plate.
2. Beat the egg in a bowl. Add the sugar and vanilla extract and mix well. Add the apples and mix well. Add the flour, cinnamon, baking powder, and salt. Mix well.
3. Place the batter in the prepared pie plate, spread the batter around, and bake for 25 to 30 minutes.

Pound Cake

There's nothing explicitly low-cal about this cake. But even so, there's only ½ tablespoon of butter per serving. I tried making this with whole wheat flour, but it just doesn't work.

This is now a foolproof recipe, using ingredients you probably already have in the house. It firmly debunks all the myths that would have you believe that you don't have the time to make things from scratch. It takes only 5 minutes from decision to putting the batter in the oven, and 40 minutes later a fabulous cake is yours. It is neutral enough to accept any kind of ice cream, fruit topping, or sauce, but it really does not need anything at all. Perfect with a quiet cup of tea. Serves 16.

8 tablespoons (one stick) unsalted butter
1 cup light brown sugar
3 eggs
1 cup 2 percent milk
1 teaspoon vanilla extract
1 teaspoon almond extract
2 cups unbleached all-purpose flour
2 teaspoons baking powder

1. Preheat the oven to 350° F. Grease and butter a 9-inch-square pan.
2. Pour the butter and sugar into a food processor fitted with the steel blade and mix until smooth. Add the eggs and mix well. Add the milk and vanilla and almond extracts and mix again. Add the flour and baking powder and process the batter until smooth.
3. Pour the batter into the prepared pan and bake for 40 minutes, or until a wooden toothpick inserted in the middle comes out clean.
4. Let the cake cool in the pan for 10 minutes. Run a spatula around the edge, to loosen the cake a bit, then invert onto a plate and cool further.

Variations

- Make a Vanilla Pound Cake: Simply omit the almond extract and increase the vanilla extract to 2 teaspoons.
- Turn this into an Orange Pound Cake: Instead of milk, substitute orange juice and use 1½ teaspoons orange extract instead of the almond extract.

Apple Crisp

This is a great all-American dessert, and it's easy to make a bit extra and have it on hand for tomorrow. Almost all fruits can go into a "crisp," but remember that if you use berries, the result will be a little more mushy.

Apple crisp is just as delicious cold as it is hot. You will need a plastic container with a secure cover to transport it for lunch. Serves 6.

6 to 8 apples, peeled, cored, and sliced
⅔ cup light brown sugar
½ cup whole wheat flour
½ cup rolled oats
½ teaspoon ground cinnamon
¼ teaspoon ground cloves
⅓ cup unsalted butter, softened, in pieces

1. Preheat oven to 375° F. Grease a shallow 1½-quart casserole.
2. Layer the apples in the casserole.
3. Pour the sugar, flour, oats, cinnamon, and cloves in a food processor fitted with the steel blade. Process until the oatmeal flakes are about half their original size.
4. Add the softened butter to the sugar-flour mixture and blend well. Sprinkle the mixture over the apples. If the mixture is in a large ball, just drop the batter a tablespoon at a time over the apples.
5. Bake the apple dish for about 30 minutes. Serve hot, warm, or cold.

Variations

- Other fruits to try in a crisp, alone or in combination, are peaches, pears, apricots, blueberries, or plums.
- You can sprinkle a few raisins or other little pieces of dried fruits over the cake.

Bread Pudding

This is one of my favorite desserts to make and eat. I imagine that it was first made by a frugal and inventive mom, from stale bread that was almost thrown away. Serves 9.

6 slices stale whole grain bread
1 cup low-fat milk
2 eggs
⅓ cup light brown sugar
1 teaspoon vanilla extract
½ teaspoon ground cinnamon
¼ cup raisins

1. Preheat the oven to 350° F. Butter a 9-inch-square pan.
2. In a large bowl tear the bread into small, 1-inch-square pieces. Pour the milk over the bread and let it stand for 30 minutes.
3. Meanwhile in a bowl place the eggs, sugar, vanilla extract, and cinnamon. Mix well. Pour over the soaked bread. Sprinkle the raisins over all and mix well.
4. Pour the bread mixture into the prepared pan, and spread it out evenly. Bake the bread pudding for 30 minutes. Serve hot, warm, or cold.

Kugel

Here's a comfort food if there ever was one! Traditionally this dish is made with egg noodles, but in truth you can use any kind of cooked pasta. Kugel is a great way to use up leftover pasta, so you might even want to make some extra noodles for dinner. The recipe can easily be doubled. Serves 2.

1 cup light sour cream
1 egg
¼ cup reduced-fat cream cheese
¼ cup light brown sugar
1 teaspoon vanilla extract
1 cup cooked noodles
¼ cup golden raisins

1. Preheat the oven to 350° F. Grease a 1½-quart dish.
2. In a blender combine the sour cream, egg, cream cheese, sugar, and vanilla. Blend until smooth.
3. In a large bowl combine the sour cream mixture, noodles, and raisins. Pour into the prepared oven dish. Bake for 50 minutes.
4. Serve hot, warm, or cold.

Rice Pudding

Once I made rice pudding with basmati rice, I never went back to white rice. The delicious taste beats plain white rice by a mile. This recipe yields about two servings, but you can double or triple the amounts with no problem. You will end up with a very creamy pudding, which will become stiff when cold, and, therefore, will transport easily for lunch in a tightly closed container. Serves 2.

½ cup white basmati rice
1 cup water
1 cup 2 percent milk
¼ teaspoon vanilla extract
⅛ teaspoon almond extract
3 tablespoons light brown sugar

1. In a small saucepan bring the rice, water, and milk to a boil over gentle heat. Turn down the heat and simmer, uncovered, for 20 to 25 minutes, stirring frequently to prevent scorching.
2. Immediately add the vanilla and almond extracts and stir well. Stir in the sugar.
3. Serve hot, warm, or cool.

Drinks

If your child is used to drinking very sweet beverages with meals, switching him or her to a different drink with less sugar will not be easy. There are many fabulous alternatives, of course, but the "hit" you get from sugar coursing through your veins is addictive. This chapter offers many alternatives, but if an attachment to sugary drinks continues to be a real stumbling block, check out the suggested literature in the Resources at the end of the book. The more you know about the damage that is done by sodas and other drinks high in sugar, the more arguments and determination you will have to entice your child to change.

As far as vegetable drinks go, your best bets will be tomato juice and commercial mixed vegetable juices. Homemade carrot juice is delicious and very nutritious, but it takes a juicer and a lot of time and carrots (about a pound per cup of juice). If you do prepare fresh vegetable juices, you will most likely already be familiar with the great blends you can make, and experimenting with your child can be fun.

Warm Apple Cider

Apple juice, like all other juices, is full of sugar. Yes, of course, it is a natural sugar, but a cup of apple juice still has about 100 calories in it that come from sugars. A fine treat but not good for a regular drink.

Still, freshly squeezed apple cider, cold and hot, is one of the joys of fall and a delicious treat. Cold apple cider needs no embellishment. But warm apple cider can be dressed up nicely, if you feel like it. As always, be sure that you do not give your child very hot things in a thermos to drink. A busy lunch table situation is not a good time to be attentive to such dangers, and your child can easily burn his or her mouth on a hot beverage. Makes 1 cup.

1 cup apple cider
1 teaspoon lemon juice
Sprinkle of ground cinnamon

In a small saucepan combine all the ingredients and heat them through until warm but not hot. Place the warm cider in a preheated thermos and seal tightly.

Iced Herbal Tea

Herbal iced tea might be one of the tricks you can use to wean a kid from the habit of wanting sugary sweet drinks. The fruit-flavored teas will probably be your best bets, and when you make the tea yourself, you can control the amount of sweetener, if any, you want to add. You can also sweeten the tea with a little honey, fruit juice, or frozen, unsweetened fruit juice concentrate. To boost the flavor, add a drop of flavor extract to the tea.

Don't for a moment think all this will really fool your child. It will not taste as sweet as a soda or a fruit drink, and it will not deliver the adrenaline boost he or she is used to. It will also not make your child's system crash later, of course, but that is not an easy connection to make. Your best hope is to sell this drink as the adult, and therefore cool, thing to do.

The reason for using herbal as opposed to regular teas is that herbal teas are naturally caffeine free. There are many fun combinations on the market, so you can experiment with several different kinds. Some flavors you and your child might like are: apple, chamomile (a very mild taste but takes a little getting used to), cranberry, lavender (little taste but great smell), lemon, mint, peach, and raspberry. Makes 1 cup.

1 to 2 herbal tea bags

Dunk the tea bags in 8 ounces of boiling water for 5 minutes. Remove the tea bags, cool the tea, and then chill it in the refrigerator. Sweeten, if desired, with honey, fruit juice, or fruit juice concentrate to taste.

Variations

- For chamomile tea, try a drop of mint or orange extract.
- For peach tea, try a drop of almond or vanilla extract.
- For cranberry tea, add a drop of orange extract.
- For lemon tea, add a drop of orange extract.
- To boost the flavor of mint tea, you can add a drop of mint extract.
- To boost the flavor of lemon tea, you can add a drop of lemon extract.

Lemonade

This is the most refreshing hot weather drink, and it is most delicious if made fresh. This is also the only way to really control the amount of sugar in the drink, which, in the commercial varieties, is considerable. Though you will get a more uniform result if you first make a sugar syrup, this version works perfectly well. If you have some water boiling for a different reason anyway, you might want to dissolve the sugar in ½ cup boiling water first, and then add the cold water and the lemon juice. Makes 1 cup.

1 cup water
3 tablespoons sugar
1½ tablespoons freshly squeezed lemon juice

Mix the ingredients well and chill. Stir again before serving.

Variation

- For a nice change in taste, sweeten the lemonade with undiluted fruit juice concentrate.

Carole's Fruit Juice Drink

Here's a great fruit drink your kids can make. Be sure to tell them to shake it up before drinking. Serves 1.

1 very ripe banana
6 strawberries
½ cup apple juice

Combine all the ingredients in a blender and mix well. Serve very cold in a thermos. Shake before drinking.

Carob Milk

Chocolate milk is a classic drink that can use some updating. If your child is African American, Native American, or Asian American, you might want to see if he or she is allergic to, or intolerant of, milk and other dairy products, a common problem in the body chemistry of these ethnic groups. You might also suspect an intolerance or allergy if your child has a lot of respiratory problems (drippy nose for months at a time, recurring ear infections, asthma). A competent allergist or nutritionist can help you with that. If your child seems to complain frequently of a tummy ache after a glass of milk, a bowl of ice cream, or a cheese sandwich, this is also an issue to bring up with your pediatrician. If you do choose to eliminate dairy, be sure to use an enriched substitute that has added calcium, or ask your pediatrician for advice. Meanwhile, there are loads of alternatives. Soy, rice, and almond milk are delicious vegetarian alternatives to cow's milk. Goat and sheep's milk are harder to find but might be tolerated when cow's milk is not.

The alternative to chocolate is the naturally sweet carob, which does not contain the caffeine-like substances that chocolate has, and it does supply a modest amount of calcium. Carob milk looks like chocolate milk and it has a small taste resemblance to it, but make no mistake: It is a different drink. If you are smart and your child is young, you'll start him or her on carob milk early.

Make the carob syrup well ahead of time, so that a cold glass of "chocolate milk" is just moments away. The trick to making a really good carob-milk drink is to mix it really well and to serve it really cold. Makes 1 cup.

To make Carob Syrup

1 cup water

1 cup powdered carob

Pour the water into a small pan and sift the carob over and into the water. Over low heat, bring the mixture to a boil, stirring constantly. Cook for about 5 minutes until the syrup is smooth. Cool and store the syrup in a covered container in the refrigerator.

To make the milk

1 cup cold milk—cow, soy, rice, or almond

1 tablespoon carob syrup

Honey to taste

In a blender process all the ingredients until smooth. Serve cold.

Variations

- Make Carob Mint Milk: Add two drops of mint extract to the milk before blending.
- For Carob Almond Milk, use almond milk and add two drops of almond extract before blending.
- Prepare Carob Peanut Butter Milk: Add a tablespoon of peanut butter and blend until smooth. Drink immediately.

Resources

There are many books, Web sites, and organizations that you can turn to for help in finding a way to help balance your family's nutritional and health habits. This is a list of sites and books that I like. You can use it as a starting point, but a short Web search will give you lots more.

For Parents

Books

Heber, David, Ph.D., M.D. *What Color Is Your Diet?* New York: HarperCollins, 2002.

> Americans eat a high-fat, highly processed "beige diet," so they need to eat more colorful fruits and vegetables. David Heber explains what specific nutrients are in groups of fruits and vegetables, and why they are necessary for our health. Recipes are included.

Heller, Richard, et al. *Carbohydrate-Addicted Kids: Help Your Child or Teen Break Free of Junk Food and Sugar Cravings—for Life!* New York: HarperCollins, 1998.

> This book explains how to figure out if your child is addicted to carbohydrates. It presents two different programs to help break the addiction to junk food. Recipes are included.

Mazel, Judy; John E. Monaco; and Sheila Sobell. *Slim & Fit Kids—Raising Healthy Children in a Fast-Food World.* Deerfield Beach, Fla.: Health Communications, 1999.

> This book was written with the cooperation of a pediatrician and was tested by many parents and their children. It tackles the issue from all angles, from digestion to exercise.

Meyerowitz, Steve. *Sprouts The Miracle Food: The Complete Guide to Sprouting.* Great Barrington, Mass.: Sproutman Publications, 2001.

> Sprouts are easy to grow, and they are a fun and very nutritious food to eat. Steve, who's known as the Sproutman, has written a book filled with great information and light humor.

Schlosser, Eric. *Fast Food Nation: The Dark Side of the All-American Meal.* New York: HarperCollins, 2002.

A thorough but very readable history of fast food in America. It will certainly make you think twice about eating in fast-food restaurants, and it will give you some background in how America's eating habits got so out of control.

Small, Eric, M.D. *Kids & Sports: Everything You and Your Child Need To Know.* New York: Newmarket Press, 2002.

This book, written by one of only eight pediatric sports specialists in the United States, gives information about children and the appropriate participation in sports at their different age levels.

Sothern, Melinda S. *Trim Kids: The Proven 12-Week Plan That Has Helped Thousands of Children Achieve a Healthier Weight.* New York: HarperResource, 2001.

Exercise physiologist Sothern, research psychologist T. Kristian Von Almen, and clinical dietician Heidi Schumacher have put together a 12-week process (beginning with a trip to your child's pediatrician) to help your child lose weight. It was developed over the last fifteen years at Louisiana State University.

Services, Web Sites, Games

Keepkidshealthy.com

This Web site is designed as a "Pediatrician's guide to your children's health and safety." It supplements the information that you receive from your child's physician, with a special emphasis on better health through preventive care. The site offers free parenting advice, on-line forums, information on product recalls, and regularly updated pediatric news.

Nutritionandkids.net.

Nutrition and Kids Adventures is a CD-ROM game for elementary school–age children designed to help kids teach themselves about proper nutrition, healthier foods, and having a healthy body.

SHAPEDOWN.com

SHAPEDOWN, a weight management program for children and adolescents, was developed by faculty members of the University of California, San Francisco, School of Medicine and includes contributions from nutrition, exercise physiology, endocrinology, psychology, family therapy, adolescent medicine, family medicine, and behavioral and developmental pediatrics.

www.bcm.tmc.edu/cnrc

The Children's Nutrition Research Center, a cooperative venture between Baylor College of Medicine, Texas Children's Hospital, and the U.S. Department of Agriculture/Agricultural Research Service (USDA/ARS), is dedicated to defining the nutrient needs of children, from conception through adolescence, as well as the needs of pregnant women and nursing mothers. On the Web site are hundreds of articles on topics ranging from helping children develop healthy eating habits to nutrition for vegetarian teens.

For Children and Teenagers

Books

American Heart Association, et al. *American Heart Association Kids' Cookbook: All Recipes Made by Real Kids in Real Kitchens!* New York: Crown Publishing Group, 1993.

Good illustrations, recipes for Garden Patch Soup and Confetti Stuffed Tomato Boats.

Cobb, Vicki. *Science Experiments You Can Eat,* rev. ed. New York: HarperTrophy, 1994.

A fun book for ages four to eight. What makes popcorn pop and how do bacteria make yogurt?

Kite, Patricia. *Gardening Wizardry for Kids.* Hauppauge, N.Y.: Barron's Educational Series, 1995.

A book filled with history, science experiments, and gardening information for reading level ages four to eight.

Lovejoy, Sharon. *Roots, Shoots, Buckets and Boots: Gardening Together with Children.* New York: Workman Publishing Company, 1999.

From watching a seed sprout to planting a pizza garden, practical information as well as the magic of gardening for kids ages nine to twelve.

Miller, Jay. *American Indian Foods: A True Book.* Danbury, Conn.: Scholastic Library Publishing, 1997.

This book for readers age four to eight discusses some of the foods Native Americans grow and gather.

O'Brien-Palmer, Michelle, and Fran Lee. *Healthy Me: Fun Ways to Develop Good Health and Safety Habits.* Chicago: Chicago Review Press, 1999.

This is a hands-on science activity book for children ages five to eight to promote health and safety through creative projects, recipes, and experiments.

Pratt, Dianne, and Janet Winter. *Hey Kids! You're Cookin' Now: A Global Awareness Cooking Adventure.* Salisbury Cove, Maine: Harvest Hill Press, 1998.

This cookbook for reading level ages nine to twelve is like reading a science book in the kitchen and cooking something at the same time.

Raab, Evelyn. *Clueless in the Kitchen: A Cookbook for Teens.* Westport, Conn.: Firefly Books, 1998.

This book for teens offers upbeat advice and easy-to-make recipes with good results.

Raymond, Carole. *Student's Vegetarian Cookbook: Quick, Easy, Cheap, and Tasty Vegetarian Recipes.* Roseville, Calif.: Prima Publishing, 2000.

If your teen wants to become a vegetarian, this is a good beginning cookbook.

Walker, Barbara M. *The Little House Cookbook: Frontier Foods from Laura Ingalls Wilder's Classic Stories.* New York: HarperCollins Children's Books, 1989.

> Sweet stories and old-fashioned recipes; kids who read the series would love this book. Reading level: ages nine to twelve.

Wilkes, Angela. *Children's Step-by-Step Cookbook*. New York: DK Publishing, Inc, 2001.

> Pure ingredients, clear photographs, and good nutrition are observed in this cookbook for reading level ages nine to twelve.

Services, Web Sites, Games

fitnessandkids.com

This comprehensive commercial site dedicated to teaching children the importance of fitness and proper nutrition features articles as well as equipment, videos, etc.

Index

C

D

E

F

About the Author

Miriam Jacobs was born in Montevideo, where her Dutch father managed a factory for Phillips Electronics. By the time she was a young adult, she had lived in urban Uruguay, rural India, on a kibbutz in Israel, and at home in Holland. She came to America and settled in New York City, where she graduated from Brooklyn College with a major in dance.

Adapting quickly to the United States, Miriam fell temporarily in love with fast food; for balance, she swallowed lots of vitamin pills. When she became pregnant with her first child, it occurred to her that she could not feed her baby this way, so she started reading Adelle Davis books and improving her choice in foods. Her first true culinary inspiration came from *The Vegetarian Epicure* by Anna Thomas, and by making her first authentic Canard à l'Orange. Miriam then taught herself to cook by reading shelffuls of cookbooks and by trying many cuisines and dishes. Now, decades later, having collected hundreds of cookbooks, she is still known to find holes in her collection and to need to acquire "just one more" cookbook.

Miriam raised and fed her three children, Sarah, Abigail, and Adam, in the Berkshire Hills in western Massachusetts. Her kids were introduced to foreign tastes early on, which may explain why all three of them have become world travelers.

She wrote recipe, food history, and cookbook review columns for a decade for two Berkshire regional publications, *Homestyle* magazine and the *Independent* newspaper. For Berkshire House, Publishers, Miriam wrote *Best Recipes of Berkshire Chefs* and did the recipe testing for *The Red Lion Inn Cookbook.* She also tested and invented recipes for a product called quark, an alternative to crème fraîche. For Storey Publishing, Miriam wrote *The 10% Low Fat Cookbook, Cooking with Soy,* and *Cooking With Edible Flowers.*

Lately her writing has turned to murder mysteries, and though nobody has gotten poisoned yet, some of her friends have become a bit reluctant about eating at her table.

Miriam now lives on the Gulf Coast in Florida, where she walks on the beach, samples fresh fish, and continues to cook new things.